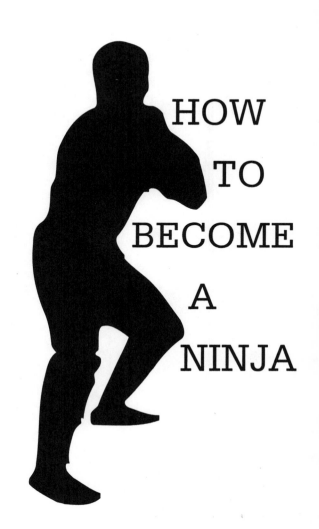

HOW
TO
BECOME
A
NINJA

SO-ACO-538

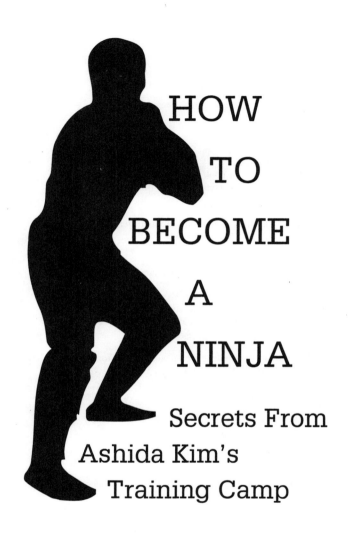

HOW
TO
BECOME
A
NINJA

Secrets From
Ashida Kim's
Training Camp

Anonymous

A Citadel Press Book
Published by Carol Publishing Group

Carol Publishing Group Edition, 1995

Previously published as *The Making of a Ninja: Ashida Kim's Training Camp*

A Citadel Press Book
Published by Carol Publishing Group
Citadel Press is a registered trademark of Carol Communications, Inc.

Editorial Offices: 600 Madison Avenue, New York, NY 10022
Sales & Distribution Offices: 120 Enterprise Avenue, Secaucus, NJ 07094
In Canada: Canadian Manda Group, One Atlantic Avenue, Suite105
Toronto, Ontario, M6K 3E7

Queries regarding rights and permissions should be addressed to:
Carol Publishing Group, 600 Madison Avenue, New York, NY 10022

Manufactured in the United States of America
10 9 8 7 6 5 4 3 2 1

Carol Publishing Group books are available at special discounts
for bulk purchases, sales promotions, fund raising, or
educational purposes. Special editions can also be created to
specifications. For details contact: Special Sales Department,
Carol Publishing Group, 120 Enterprise Ave., Secaucus, NJ 07094

Neither the author nor the publisher assumes any responsibility
for the use or misuse of information contained in this book.

Library of Congress Cataloging-in-Publication Data

How to become a Ninja: secrets from Ashida Kim's training camp / by
    Anonymous.
       p.   cm.
    "A Citadel Press book."
    ISBN 0-8065-1558-9 (pbk.)
    1. Ninjutsu.
UB271.J3H69   1995
355.5'4—dc20   94-44943
                                                   CIP

Contents

Foreword

I applied for acceptance to Ashida Kim's training camp at the request of the grandmaster of a rival Ninja clan. As a secret agent of that organization, I was assigned to infiltrate a special training session hosted by Kim and, with the knowledge I would acquire, later sabotage his entire operation.

"And while you're at it," instructed the grandmaster as I set out, "find out once and for all who this Ashida Kim really is!"

As a result of my participation in this class, however, I gradually began to realize that the grandmaster had been motivated by petty jealousy of Kim and his unique style rather than by his stated idealistic belief that Kim was leading astray those who came to him for training.

Consequently, albeit with great hesitation and—yes—fear, I finally confessed my part in the plot to Kim's chief instructor and volunteered my services to Kim's organization. The following is my chronicle of the events that transpired during my training, an elaborate and detailed journal relating to the techniques and methods taught at Kim's camp. With the permission and assistance of Kim's staff of instructors I have polished, compiled, and published my daily notes in order to dispel the false rumors that circulate about Kim's organization and to give those who desire to know about ninjitsu a glimpse of this esoteric world.

Publisher's Note

Although the nature of his assignment made it impossible for the author to photograph specific techniques or locations, we have prevailed upon the services of Ashida Kim and his staff of instructors to assist us in illustrating those methods taught at the training base that they were willing to reveal.

All references to landmarks as well as descriptions of the students and teachers who took part have been deleted so that their identities and anonymity may be preserved; and political and geographical details that pertain to security of operations currently in progress have been removed.

Participation in such a training experience is by invitation only, and one must already be qualified in another system before being considered eligible to apply. Even so, all martial arts teach these secrets at the advanced levels; all must be learned one step at a time.

The Welcome

He was a small Oriental man with broad shoulders, and I noticed that he wore an ancient puzzle ring on his left hand, marking him as a member of the secret society. Watchful, alert, betraying no emotion, his eyes seemed to scan the assemblage. As he descended the oaken staircase of the stately country home, the soft and well-worn carpet cushioned his step. I doubted that he would have been heard at any rate, so light was his tread; and the low murmur of conversation among the couples and small groups below him also covered his approach. As he paused, just above the foot of the stair, most of the others were still unaware of his presence, and even those standing closest to him were startled when he spoke.

"Ladies and gentlemen," he began, without discernable accent. Like many another charismatic speaker, he had a voice which, while seemingly quiet, easily carried to the far side of the parlor, where I stood. The group's jovial after-dinner mood turned serious as each member focused his attention upon the speaker; but he waited, unmoving, for complete silence before continuing.

"I am to be your chief instructor. Permit me to welcome you to the House of Two Moons, headquarters for the next phase of your training." He began to stroll easily among the students.

"You have been selected from your various teams and units because you have passed the various tests that qualify you for participation in this program," he told the group. "Here, you will learn many new things and acquire special skills that will enable you to survive in the field, and in the world of men. You will become Ninja!"

He looked into every face, as if memorizing each, or searching for some hidden answer; I felt that his intense gaze probed the mind. His voice never wavered, nor did his glance linger long enough to cause discomfort. Each student listened intently, as if the words were meant for him.

"Over six thousand years ago, Sun Tze, in his classic work, *The Art of War,* stated quite clearly that the key to victory lies not in devastating the enemy—for this leads to bitterness and revenge—but rather in keeping the peace. All life is precious, and no life can be replaced.

"The Sage instructed that in order to keep the peace, the Emperor must have knowledge of any plans and plots hatching against him to forestall an attack or challenge to his authority before it could develop sufficiently to become a significant threat. This was the beginning of the great game of espionage, the most thankless and dangerous trade ever devised; and the most important to the empire. Sun Tze taught that anyone, even the most lowly and despised, can be a valuable source of information.

"Therefore, befriend the disgruntled, be liberal with bribes and favors, and treat everyone with respect. In this way you may penetrate unseen into the inner sanctum of the enemy's camp and discover his most closely guarded secrets. This is the meaning of the old saying, 'The king has one thousand eyes.'

"Ninjitsu is an honorable profession, bound by a code of ethics as rigid as that of the samurai."

Having circumnavigated the room, the speaker began to ascend the staircase, then looked back over his shoulder at the group.

"Some of you may learn it; those who do will be changed forever." He turned a bit more.

"I need not remind you of the need for secrecy. What you see here, what is said here, when you leave, let it stay here. The Ninja warrior travels incognito. No one can be trusted, nothing can be believed, and"—he smiled—"anything is possible."

The group remained attentive as he continued. "Train hard, learn much. In this way, you may learn the truth for yourself." His lip curled slightly and his eyes twinkled briefly.

"Sleep well, my young friends. We begin at dawn. Good night." And with that he placed a hand on the bannister and climbed the stairs.

We all relaxed after his departure. Even though his speech had been neither intimidating nor frightening, the undercurrent of tension which this unusual individual had brought into the room seemed to dissipate with his exit, and I felt relief spread like a cool breeze among the trainees. Somewhere far away there was the sound of a door closing quietly, the latch clicking into place.

After signing ourselves in—there was a large bound ledger for this purpose—we left the House of Two Moons and retired to the bunkhouse for the night.

The training camp was located on the north fork of a small river, and was surrounded by 8,000 acres of pine and hardwood forest. It lay approximately eighteen miles north of the rural airport. The area was covered with creek bottoms, soybean fields, and a 1,000-acre green pasture. Game was plentiful and the area was heavily populated with deer and turkey, as well as quail and small game like rabbit and squirrel.

The bunkhouse was about four miles from the main highway, along an old gravel road which twisted and wound through the woodland hills. It had a large living room, an enclosed dining and recreation area, a bathroom, one large bunk room, and one bedroom. Ten to twelve people could sleep there comfortably. There were air conditioners throughout, and the rooms were furnished with space heaters for winter. The kitchen was equipped with an electric stove, a refrigerator with ice maker, and hot and cold running water.

Each member of our training group was assigned a bunk, and on each bunk lay a black plastic bag, sealed with tape, containing the following: a coverall garment of drab color, selected to fit the individual; a full-coverage black hood with eye holes; and a pair of ankle-high tabi boots.

Enclosed with these articles was a typewritten note which read, "Please accept this uniform as the official dress of the camp. The coverall is a disposable garment designed to be discarded once the agent has penetrated enemy territory. Thereafter, he would wear clothing appropriate to the terrain and locale. It should be worn as an oversuit, to protect and conceal whatever other costume is worn. Furthermore, when all of the members of the class are dressed and masked alike it will be difficult for the enemy to ascertain the size of our force and to identify its individual members. This is

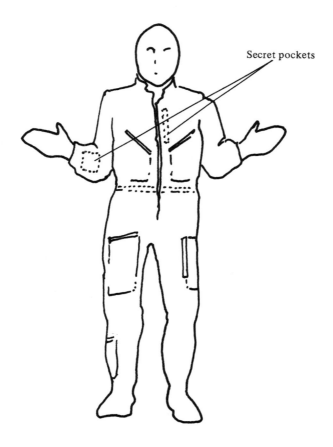

Secret pockets

Figure 1. Uniform issued at Ninja camp with interior and exterior pockets.

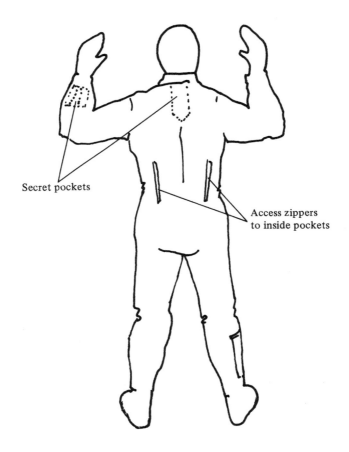

Secret pockets

Access zippers
to inside pockets

Figure 1A. Rear view of pocket placement.

called blending into the crowd. The color and pattern of the
material are designed to camouflage the agent in the forest.

"The various pockets of the coverall are designed to hold
those items necessary for the mission, as well as to carry and
conceal devices and tools useful to the solitary agent [Figure
1]. The hood is customarily carried in the left waist pocket;
arm and leg pockets may be used for shuriken or knives. The
boots will make it easy to walk quietly and quickly."

Day One

The next morning before first light, each of the new recruits was quietly awakened by a gentle touch on the left shoulder. After washing up, we were cautioned to silence and led, sleepy-eyed, to the dewy, grass-covered training field. There we were arranged in roughly straight rank-and-file rows facing east.

The members of the group had been selected from widely differing sources. All of us were volunteers for this special training, yet apparently no two had ever met before. We sat for what seemed a very long time, cross-legged, backs straight, heads up.

Finally one trainee, a burly young man who looked like a football player, leaned toward me, introduced himself as "Jake," and whispered, "What are we doing?"

Relaxed, enjoying the cool morning air, I was slow to reply. "Waiting," I said softly, when it appeared the questioner was on the verge of asking again.

"For what?"

"For something wonderful to happen." I made a slight movement to draw his attention to the sunrise.

RUNNING

The rosy dawn crept over the horizon—at first just a few rays, then a warming glow and a fiery orb rising majestically. As it climbed, I imagined that each heart was filled with new hope and resolve that it should be the one who passed the tests ahead to succeed where lesser beings failed.

"Dawn," began the resonant voice of the chief instructor, "is a time of great energy. The sun warms the earth with its power; like twilight, it is a magical time, during which the Force may be absorbed and circulated within the body."

His voice seemed to be coming from everywhere and nowhere at once, yet forceful. Faced with an ever increasing intensity of light, most of the students had closed their eyes which doubtless added to the hypnotic effect. The tempo of his speech encouraged slow and rhythmic breathing.

"The Earth permits all, high and low, rich or poor, to sit upon her equally, without falling away; the Sun shines freely on all without discrimination. Imagine a spot two inches below your naval; this is your center, your *hara,* the meeting of heaven and earth.

"War is essentially a matter of breath control, both among the politicians who start wars and the soldiers who must die in them. Victory lies not in which side is right or wrong, or even in which is more powerful, for desire alone will often win in spite of superior arms or numbers. The key lies in stamina. The combatant that tires of the conflict first allows the other to deliver the deciding stroke and claim victory. This is the lesson of history and all martial arts. Part of your goal will be to make the enemy tire of battle by disrupting his activities. Since much of this assignment would be carried out in enemy territory, and since many of you will be training for HALO (High Altitude/Low Opening) parachute insertion, it is vitally important that we begin to develop your wind, stamina, and the strength of your legs and ankles.

"To this end, the ancients devised a most perfect exercise. It is called running. In the past a Ninja could travel over eighty miles a day by means of special techniques developed over years of practice.

"The secret to long-distance running is to build and reduce speed slowly. Remember, running is an altered state of being; eventually one must return to a more normal pace and fade into the crowd to vanish.

"If you will please rise, we will begin the warm-up exercises that will prevent over-exertion of the muscles and tendons so that we may concentrate on building stamina."

The class stood slowly and followed him through an elaborate series of preparatory stretching movements. He continued to address them as they worked.

"Many people run on their heels. This has a jarring effect on the internal organs and may cause permanent injury. The long-distance runner runs on the ball of the foot; his heel never touches the ground. His ankle acts as a shock absorber and provides an extra spring to the step. Many boxers hold their rear heel up in order to achieve the same effect. This is not the only way to run, but is useful for our purposes."

The exercises were standard calisthenics. We moved from slow neck rotations, shoulder shrugs, trunk rotations, and toe-touching to push-ups, sit-ups, and kneebends, and ended with deep breathing, arms describing a large circle out and upward from hips to above the head for inhalation, back down for exhalation. The chief instructor had told us to close our eyes to enhance the visual experience of drawing the energy into the body.

"Open your eyes now and look at the horizon. Keep watching it as you run. When you feel tired, press the first joint of your index finger with the thumb."

The drill instructor now took charge of the group. He was a totally different type of teacher from the calm, soft-spoken chief instructor. His face spread into a wide grin as he stepped in front of the assembled recruits. From his scarred and wizened visage a long history of training men could be read. Planting his feet wide apart and digging his fists into his waistband, he spoke in a commanding tone.

"Right! Now that you little boys and girls have had your morning nap, welcome to the real world. Those of you who know me are aware of the type of treatment you can expect. Those of you who have not had the pleasure of my company before would do well to observe the fear in the face and tremor in the voice of the more experienced among you.

"Sensei—" he bowed in the direction of the chief instructor—"is most kind and polite. I am not so. You must run as if your life depends on it, for it someday may. I will tolerate no slackers. Anyone who drops out during the first mile will be immediately cut from the program. Any who fall out during subsequent miles will be beaten senseless and left where they lie. In the Legion we had a saying: 'march or die'; here it is the same. If you drop out, I will beat you. If you turn back, I will beat you. If you fall down unconscious and die, I will beat you. It will give me the greatest pleasure." He smiled menacingly.

We ran for what seemed an eternity. Many were gasping for breath long before we reached the first mile marker along the packed dirt road upon which we traveled, but none dared drop out.

True to his word, the drill instructor fell back and began verbally and physically intimidating those not meeting his standard of calisthenic performance.

In sharp contrast, the chief instructor, always supportive, ran easily back and forth between the members of the group, encouraging those who seemed to be flagging and offering a word of advice to those in distress and a helping hand to those stumbling to keep up.

As the course wore on, the experienced runners began to hit their stride, and several of us found the pace to be somewhat slower than our individual norms. Endorphins racing through my system, I soon developed a runner's high and started noticing the beauty of the landscape.

Near the forefront ran a striking Oriental girl who could scarcely have been more than twenty years old.There were other women in the class (all of them billeted in separate quarters in the House of Two Moons), but she was by far the youngest and most attractive. The others, far less feminine, could easily be identified by their marching gait as members of the armed forces.

The girl ran easily, breathing deeply through her nose, her long black hair trailing out behind her like a ribbon or scarf. With each step she sprang forward like a deer bounding through the primeval forest.

Several others of us also seemed unperturbed by the physical exertion, including Jake, the young man with whom I had earlier held the whispered conversation concerning the nature of the sunrise meditation. He was large and muscular, and his relentless dogtrot was characteristic of a jogger. Occasionally he had trouble with some aberration of terrain, such as a pothole or a stretch of uneven turf; the sandy, hard-packed soil seemed less suited to his pace than would the asphalt of some suburban road. Due to my cross-country training, I had little difficulty compensating for the changing conditions and obstacles.

After the third mile mark, even some of the recruits in better shape and with more experience began to tire. After five had fallen by the wayside, the chief instructor made his way to the front of the column and gradually slowed the pace to a trot and then a fast walk which subsided into a more normal marching step.

Passing between two large boulders, he raised his hand to call a halt, and the class collapsed mercifully to the ground. Even though we had had a cool-down procedure, a few recruits crawled away to heave loudly, no doubt thankful that there had been no morning meal to put extra strain on the body. As we sat, all of us panting heavily, some trying in vain to catch their breath, the chief instructor passed from one to another, rewarding each for his or her efforts and success at making it this far. We recovered more quickly after this and sat quietly acknowledging his praise as our fallen comrades gradually rejoined the group. Eventually the yells and screams of the drill instructor could be heard, and soon we were all together again.

"Stamina," said the chief instructor, "is the key. Ninja must be able to travel great distances in a short time without leaving a trail. This is important when escaping as well as infiltrating.

"Take cover!" The sudden command hissed across the small clearing, animating even the most weary to instant action. Within seconds, the rustling of the surrounding shrubbery died away and the area was as empty as if no one had passed that way for some time. We crouched breathlessly, quietly straining to catch some hint of the cause for alarm. After a few minutes a low chuckle, emanating from some secret hiding place, seemed to mock us. Almost simultaneously came the droning sound characteristic of certain insects, and I spotted a large black and yellow striped wasp hovering menacingly over the area.

The chief instructor strode back into the clearing and

called the team to assemble in a circle around him.

"You see," he said, indicating his aerial companion, "even a tiny insect, armed only with one drop of venom, can disrupt an entire company of trained killers. This is how you must strive to be. Make the enemy hunt you everywhere. Sabotage his activities so that he can never rest. Like the wasp, unless you are near the nest, you act alone. Think of the hexagram, the six-sided figure; this is the symbol of the hive, of home. It tells the little brother you are a friend."

The chief instructor raised his hand. The wasp circled once, then landed, wings twitching.

SURVIVAL

"In the field, we must learn to be observant of everything, for even the smallest detail may be of tremendous significance in the game of life and death. Certain wasps require water for the construction of their nests. Would not a cool drink of water be refreshing?" As he looked about the group, several trainees swallowed with difficulty.

"You will notice that we have come without any sort of canteen and are quite some distance from camp. If you were an escaping prisoner, fleeing in hostile-controlled territory, one of your evasion goals would be to locate fresh potable water. Also, when infiltrating, it is advisable to establish the base camp near water.

"The Chinese sage Lu Yu declared, 'Mountain water is best, river water is next best; well water is poor. The first should be taken from springs where the water flows over a rocky bed; the second from only those parts of the river where the flow is swift.' Near the lee side, the current is too rapid, stirring up debris, soil and sand; on the far side it is sluggish, holding sediment; in the center it is clearest. Snow and rain may be used, although neither is completely pure, as well as the dew on the underside of leaves (or a plastic sheet), but the amount of moisture obtained from dew is minute.

"Finding fresh water in the wilderness is of paramount importance to survival or long-term evasion. One may locate this commodity by many methods. The smell of water carries far on a hot day, or before a storm; one may follow animal trails or insects; or a knowledge of topography may be of use in determining the most likely site."

The chief instructor now told us to sit comfortably and close our eyes. In a few minutes, the cooling forest breeze banished all fatigue, allowing us to return to a calm and meditative state. "Listen," he said softly.

At first only the wind could be heard, then the distant chirping of birds and squirrels chattering. But slowly, in the still spaces between the gentle puffs of the breeze, one could hear the distant gurgling of a cascading mountain stream. When the breeze blew, its airy caress brought from the north not only the scents of pine needles and oak, but also, ever so faintly, water.

After allowing the group sufficient time to make these observations, he instructed us to open our eyes and stand. "In the field," he whispered, "conserve water by not talking and by moving slowly and quietly. Too much exertion in the sun may cause heatstroke."

The small procession moved single file off the main trail and into the surrounding brush. We were soon following a thin path through the trees and rocks around a small knoll of ground toward a sheer rock face. As we traveled, the sound of splashing water became gradually louder until at last we came upon a mountain spring. Its waters spilled from a cavernous cleft in the wall of stone straight down into a large and silvery pool before rippling off in a brightly sparkling stream.

All were amazed that we had traveled so far to reach the destination, since the sounds that had attracted our attention had seemed much nearer.

"When searching with the mind," explained the chief instructor, "time and space have no meaning. In such cases, trust your first instinct, since the intuitive processes of the mind are most often correct."

One of the recruits suggested that a tributary of the spring might run near the main trail, and so could have been heard as the group was led along a trail parallel to, but out of sight of, the watery finger. To this the pair of instructors smiled between themselves and suggested aloud that this too might have been the case.

"In ninjitsu, anything is possible; even trickery and deception," said the drill instructor. "Why, even this water, which your comrades are preparing to drink, may be poisoned."

The more experienced of the crew, having deduced that the instructors were certainly aware of the spring's location beforehand and would not have led us to a contaminated water supply, had moved to the edge of the rocky pool, where we dipped our hands, and then wetted our faces with the cold water. That several recruits also scanned the farther bank and surrounding terrain, and had not yet taken a drink, was a credit to whatever previous training they had encountered. Some of us smiled with the masters at their private joke.

Even swiftly flowing water which appears pure can be poisoned by an abundance of natural life, the chief instructor explained. Amoebae, tiny one-celled creatures too small to be seen with the naked eye, and other protozoan microorganisms, when ingested, quickly cause debilitating dysentery and intestinal ulceration. Certain parasitic worms can also be present, as can unknown pollutants from an upstream source.

"Even stagnant, muddy, or polluted water may be drunk in an emergency," the chief instructor explained. "Water may be purified by boiling or freezing. Boiling kills microorganisms by heat and agitation; freezing solidifies pure water first, leaving toxic materials near the center. The water may be filtered through paper or ground charcoal and sand, and should be allowed to stand for half a day.

"Generally speaking, however, it is less a matter of whether the water is 'safe' than if one can safely drink it. The ancients devised a simple but effective method of chemical testing to determine the answer to this question—smell!

"Observe the cat as it drinks. It looks at the surface to judge clarity, touches the surface to check turbidity, and sniffs before partaking of the liquid. This is not taught to the cat, it is the product of generations of selective behavior producing felines which survive.

"So look, then touch the water; feel it for grittiness, or

oiliness; scoop up a handful and sniff it for any sulphur, alcohol, or sour odor. Smell in short bursts rather than a long inhalation, and waft the aroma to the nostrils carefully at first. Sift the liquid through the fingers and look for residue. Then cup the hands together and enclose the dampness between them. Blow into the hand-chamber to combine breath with water. Then check again by smell.

"Under arctic conditions, do not eat crushed ice, as this may injure the lips and tongue, or snow in its natural state, as this leads to dehydration. If necessary, pack the snow into sticks or balls before eating; but remember that if you are hot, cold, or tired, eating snow chills the body. Also, it takes about half again as much time and fuel to get a given amount of water from melting snow as from melting ice."

With his direction and the assistance of the drill instructor, the entire group practiced the method of testing the clear, ice-cold water of the pool for purity. All declared that the sparkling liquid possessed a slightly sweetish odor, not at all unpleasant. The pair of teachers confirmed this diagnosis and testified to the excellence and cleanliness of the spring and pool. Despite this assurance, neither permitted any of the students to drink.

Instead, they insisted that everyone disperse into the surrounding area and gather one piece of firewood each. With no more instruction than that, we were set to the task, and in short order had assembled a substantial pile of debris on the bank. Each piece was considered in light of its fuel potential, kindling temperature, and role in the construction of the fire. No piece was discounted nor made fun of, even the green wood brought by the neophyte. Explaining that it would provide smoke to keep away the insects, and would burn more slowly, having to dry first, the chief instructor placed the limb on the downwind side of the fire to receive and reflect heat.

Setting aside a bit of punk (dry, decayed, resinous wood) to use as tinder, he next separated the rest of the firewood into heaps of tinder, kindling, and fuel. Then, as the group huddled about him, he built a circular stack of wood and sat down cross-legged on its upwind side.

"Over the years various methods of purifying water have been devised, among them the ancient and honorable art of tea. In order to make tea," he said matter-of-factly, "one must first boil water. Fire and water are two of the four elements of nature; to boil water, one must know how to make fire." He smiled, as if this were perfectly clear and explained everything.

The activities of the morning had consumed much of the early half of the day. The sun was climbing toward its zenith, and the heat had begun to grow oppressive for those unaccustomed to heavy exertion. Still, everyone watched intently as the chief instructor stared at the sheltered pile of finely crumbled punk, which awaited only the spark that would ignite it.

Slowly he raised his hands, palms down, above the tinder. All eyes were on him and all breathing diminished in anticipation. A point of light, no larger than a pin head, appeared. It grew, receded, and grew again, dancing over the punk. A wisp of smoke arose, then a finger of flame traced a black thread over the tinder. He bent forward and blew gently on the little fire to increase its heat before adding twigs and shavings.

"White man build big fire, sit way back; Indian build little fire, sit up close. That is an old Indian saying," said the chief instructor.

"From earliest times, fire has been what separated man from the animals," he continued. "At first it was a mystery, a magic power, stolen from the gods, who dropped it from heaven in the form of lightning. The first guard duty was that of the keeper of the flame. The first shaman was the one who could produce fire at will.

"For the Ninja, fire has many uses: light, warmth, cooking, boiling water, arson. In this day and age, even a novice requires little more than an ample supply of waterproof matches in order to create an adequate blaze.

"'Strike-anywhere' or kitchen matches can easily be waterproofed by coating them with a thin layer of wax. Striking one against any rough surface—a rock, a metal button, even a thumbnail—will cut through the wax on the matchhead and produce a flame. All matches, whether or not they have been waterproofed, should always be carried in a watertight container. Many modern survival knives feature a compartment in the handle for storage in the field.

"In addition, a great variety of disposable lighters which operate on gas or lighter fluid sparked by a tiny flint and steel wheel are widely available and very functional.

"Presuming the absence of any of the various fire-starting devices such as matches or lighters, the Ninja in the field must be prepared to generate the vital spark without modern conveniences. He must rely on primitive methods.

"T'ou ch'ieh shang ti is a term which means 'stealing fire from the enemy.' If the agent is in hostile territory for the purpose of intelligence gathering or sabotage and is sufficiently adept at the art of infiltrating, he may make off with fire-making devices or even, as in olden times, a live coal.

"Very often one's ability to survive depends on the ability to make a fire. If you have only an ember, you must know how to nurse it into flame. For the purpose of practice, you may use the lit end of a cigar. To produce fire by this method one must have patience as well as tinder. This is the secret of making fire by primitive methods.

"Any material that will catch the spark and smoulder can be used as tinder. The best is dry, decayed wood, which may be found even in the dampest climates by burrowing to the heart of rotten logs. Finely shredded dry bark, powdered wood dust, lint, bird's nests, ground pine nettles, birch and pine resin, and wood shavings also make good tinder, provided they are bone-dry.

"Before starting your fire, dig a pit for it. The pit must be shallow, since fuel needs air in order to burn. Use the excavated earth to erect a windbreak to protect the fire. If the fire is to be built on wet or snow-covered ground, first make a platform upon which the fire may rest. If yours is a base camp, encircle the platform with stones to hold and reflect heat. Allow for proper ventilation; don't burn up your own air. Set the fire carefully so it will not get out of hand.

"Now you are ready to build the fire. Touch the smoldering tip of a cigar or incense stick to the tinder in your tinder-box, which should be fireproof as well as waterproof. Gently blow on or fan the material as it begins to smoke. It may take several tries to get a spark to spread and grow. Usually, this is the fault of too coarse a grade of tinder. The more dust-like it is, the better.

"Once the tinder is going, the initiate is faced with the problem of fueling the fire. Carefully and gradually add kindling, using progressively larger shavings and chips, until a flame is produced. Try it a few times. It is not as easy as it sounds. But, if you want to survive in the field, it must be learned.

"Now begin to add leaves, dried dung (in the desert), or oil if it is available to coax the feeble flame into a robust fire, and continue to feed it with twigs and branches until it has grown to the desired size. Surround your fire with green logs or large stumps. This will hold the heat and make the fuel burn more slowly.

"There are various primitive methods of starting a fire by making sparks or heat. One should be familiar with them so they may be employed if necessary.

"Friction is the most difficult means of starting a fire. Long ago in Asia a tool was invented in which a strip of bamboo was rapidly sawed back and forth in a split stick [Figure 2]. The American Indian stood one stick, or broken arrow, in a notch of firewood, looped his bowstring over it, and by this arrangement drilled the shaft into the log with sufficient speed and friction to produce not only a fine black dust capable of sustaining combustion, but also sufficient heat to ignite it [Figure 3]. When smoke begins to rise from the point of contact, remove the smoldering wood to the tinder-box.

"Probably the most universally accepted way to ignite tinder is by the use of the classical flint and steel. In an emergency, a knife blade can be made to produce a spark against a rock.

"Hold the flint, or stone, as near as you can to the tinder. Strike downward with the steel, or knife, so that any spark flies into the flammable material. Carry flint with you or experiment with surrounding rocks until you find a type

Figure 2. Early Asians rapidly sawed a strip of bamboo back and forth in a split stick to generate a spark.

Figure 3. American Indians made fire-starting less arduous by spinning a stick in a drilling motion.

which will suffice. This too, is more difficult than it sounds, but with practice it can be done.

"Soon after the advent of the magnifying lens, it was discovered that such a glass could be used to start a fire by focusing the sun's rays on some flammable material [Figure 4]. Small boys have long known the pleasure of burning their initials on wood with the beam of light.

"Fire requires three things: heat, oxygen, and fuel. The absence of any one of these makes combustion impossible.

"The Ninja method is the most efficient way to sustain a long-lived, versatile fire. It is essentially a hole, or cave, fire with a primitive chimney.

"Make the pit about ten inches deep and twelve inches across at the top, tapering to eight inches at the bottom. Dig a narrower chimney tunnel on the upwind side of the first

Figure 4. One Ninja method of fire-starting is to use a lens or magnifying glass to focus the sun's rays on the tinder.

pit and connect the two with a series of horizontal passage-ways. As the wind blows across the top of the chimney hole, air will be drawn into the larger hole to fan the fire and keep it going. This process, known as drafting, provides adequate ventilation for combustion.

"Fuel is dropped into the hearth pit until a bed of coals has been established for cooking. All of the heat produced is funneled upward for cooking. No light escapes to betray your position except that which is reflected by objects directly above the pit. If dry fuel is employed, most of the smoke will be dispersed in a manner that is unlikely to give away the camp. When the fire pit is dug at the entrance of a shelter, heat and warmth are conducted naturally to the interior. A ring of small fires of this type around a site will often provide more warmth than a large conventional camp-fire. The underground fireplace protects the fire from being extinguished or spread by the wind. Because the fire is closely contained inside the pit, it can be rapidly quenched with earth or water at the approach of an enemy.

"Miamoto Musashi, Japan's most famous swordsman, advised in his treatise on strategy and tactics that the fire should always be kept to one's right in combat. Likewise it is useful to mention that looking into the fire or any light at night will cause the pupils of the eye to constrict, reducing the amount of light that strikes the retina. This is important for the Ninja, who hides in the shadows during the day or star-gazes to accustom his eyes to the dark of night. It requires about twenty minutes for the eye to be fully adapted. Also, when the enemy looks up from the fire to see you, his eyes must first adjust to the change in light

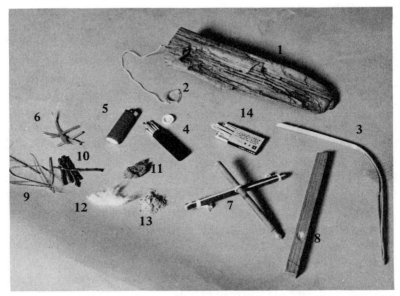

Figure 5. Fire-starting implements: 1) dry log; 2) magnifying glass; 3) bamboo strip; 4) matches in waterproof case; 5) butane lighter; 6) wood shavings (kindling); 7) shaft and drill apparatus; 8) wood block for drill; 9) bamboo fibers; 10) twigs; 11) lint; 12) cotton; 13) sawdust; 14) matches.

intensity. This provides the half-second advantage during which to strike. If guards patrol past or from a well-lit area, their night vision will also be less than optimum.

"A flash of fire, therefore, may temporarily blind a person, even if it does not burn him or make him flinch. This, of course, is the inherent danger in developing overly sensitive night vision. A sudden extinguishing of light also produces temporary blindness. A bucket of water dumped on a campfire drowns the blaze and also creates a cloud of smoke sufficient to hide one's escape or enable one to apparently materialize in the midst of the camp.

"Furthermore, fire may be used to deceive the enemy. By building many fires around a besieged city, one may mislead one's opponent into believing one's army is larger than it is. Or, when you vacate a building, leave a candle burning by the window. It will lull the enemy into a false sense of security, for he will believe you are there as long as he can see your light.

"Arson was a form of sabotage in which the ancient Ninja specialized. The lessons learned in building a fire made him acutely aware of what was flammable, and his study of architecture taught him the best places to ignite the paper and wood houses or straw huts of the period.

"The penetrating agent would often hide in attics or lofts during the night, then disrupt the enemy by setting fires when battle was launched at dawn; or he would wait until the enemy had gone out patrolling to set fires in his absence; or he might demoralize the enemy by setting fires after an apparent Ninja defeat. In any event, much of the enemy manpower would necessarily have to be spent in battling the blaze, or guarding the streets at night, in order to preserve whatever semblance of order remained and to protect reserves of food and water.

"Commandos during World War II were instructed in methods of manufacturing time-delay devices similar in many ways to the long fuse of the Ninja. One commando time-delay device was made by lighting a cigarette and then folding the cover of a matchbook over its unlit end. When the cigarette burned down to the matchbook it would ignite the matchheads, creating a fiery torch which would in turn set fire to packing crates, shredded paper, and so on.

"The ancient Ninja used slow-burning sticks of incense of different lengths as fuses. In this way, one man could set many widely spaced fires which would all ignite at about the same time. Some schools used S- or L-shaped candles for this purpose."

As the chief instructor spoke, his deft fingers had kindled a small fire which now had a glowing bed of coals, and, in the soft soil beside the pool, he had hand-dug a U-shaped stove. He shoveled the live embers to the hearth pit and then, with a few green twigs, he quickly fashioned a crude grate over the top, through which the flames could be fed.

Reaching inside his jerkin, he produced a brown paper bag. He unfolded the bag, curled its upper edges to form a collar, and handed the improvised bucket to the nearest student.

"Fill this to the rim with water from the pool," he directed, "and take care not to spill any."

The recruit hastened to perform his task and soon returned, fingers curled under the turned-down lip of the bag, which was brimming with the cold mountain water. The bag was beginning to leak, and a large drop hung quivering at its base. By the time it had been passed back to the instructor, the paper collar had started to moisten and turn a darker brown. He placed the bag on the grate. Fire licked at the bottom and sides of the brown paper cauldron, but the instructor calmly continued to drop fuel into the flames below.

The folded rim of the sack soon burned away but, despite much hissing and gurgling, the sack itself held firm.

"The water inside the bag cools the fibers of the paper, which keeps them below kindling temperature," the instructor explained. "The bag is simultaneously cooled and heated, and so remains impervious to the effects of fire or water. The twigs that form the grate are also protected by the moisture of the paper."

The cauldron now gurgled and hissed at a steady rate, an equilibrium of sorts having been reached between the forces at play. The surface of the water bubbled intermittently, suggesting that it had come to a low boil, and occasional wisps of steam served to confirm this deduction.

"Ah." The chief instructor smiled, seemingly pleased by this event. From a pocket he drew a small leather drawstring and, when the water had been boiling for about two minutes, he began to sprinkle the contents of the pouch into the brew. It appeared to be a finely ground powder of reddish hue which turned the water slightly orange. Those of us who were close enough to see into the makeshift pot watched the hypnotically swirling brew.

In a moment, the teacher passed out small origami folded paper cups. Each student was asked to note how his cup had been fashioned and instructed to dip it into the kettle to receive a cup of tea and then cover it with one hand to hold in the fragrance for the space of three breaths before drinking to allow the drink to cool and sediment to settle to the bottom.

All were welcome to drink their fill, and several took advantage of the opportunity to return for another sip of the refreshing brew. Many remarked that the experience of watching the ceremony had caused them to forget their aching muscles in concentration. The tea was stimulating, tasting of mint and orange with a lingering sweetness, almost like honey. The top of the bag had burned away as the water level fell until now, by some miracle, a little more than a frying panful remained, simmering persistently.

"All of you hold your empty cups like so." The drill instructor demonstrated. "Close your eyes and think of your mission," he ordered quietly. "Pray to succeed—" he paused—"and to live."

"Place your cups in the fire," he said after a few seconds. Each of us filed by in turn, folding his cup and dropping it through the wood grate.

When all of the cups had burned and the water boiled away into steam, leaving the soggy remains of the bag to smolder above the fire pit, the chief instructor spoke once more.

"We have performed this ceremony many times, yet each time is like the first. Now we are water brothers, just as our ancestors were centuries ago.

"Water is the symbol of love; tea is the symbol of healing. Should you find yourself with dysentery in the field, drinking tea will help to calm the mind and heal the body.

"We have often come here to perform this rite, yet you will see no evidence that we have been here before. It is in keeping with the principles of leaving no trace of our passing for the enemy to discover and of respect for Nature that we not disturb things too much.

"What Nature freely provides, the dried branches and leaves, the pure water, these we may take and use freely. But anything which is living must be considered. When the hunter shoots his game, he does not kill more than he needs; this is called economy. When the herbalist collects his teas, he thanks the tree or bush for sharing with him its essence and life-giving properties. We must always seek to restore the natural balance when it has been upset."

With that, the chief instructor pushed the mound of earth that had been removed from the fire pit back into the hole. As the remains of the bag, grate, and coals were smothered, a cloud of smoke belched from the chimney hole. He filled the chimney with another shovelful of dirt and, after he had fanned the air, it was as if no fire had ever been there.

"From now on," the chief instructor continued, "when we stop, do not sit or cross the legs, as this impedes the circulation and makes it more difficult to move swiftly. Instead, crouch by placing one knee on the ground, sit on the heel, and rest the opposite elbow on the uplifted knee [Figures 6 and 7]. If you are carrying a weapon hold it in that hand. Let the back curve naturally, and breathe slowly and quietly. Scan the horizon moving the head as little as possible, keeping alert for any movement. This is called the 'kneeling hunter stance.' Sniff the wind for scent, noting its direction and meteorological conditions. Look for game; from now on we will be hunting."

"For what?" asked a voice from the crowd.

Instantly the drill instructor started to lunge forward at the offender, but was stayed by a hand from the chief.

"For dinner," he replied calmly.

"What about lunch?" asked someone else from the rear of

Figure 6. Ninja kneeling stance. Front.

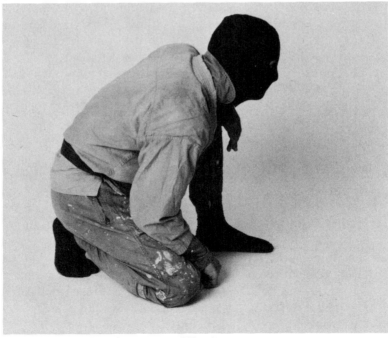

Figure 7. Ninja kneeling stance. Side view.

the group, after a moment's hesitation.

"We just finished it," was the answer, followed by a smile. "The tea," he said, looking into the incredulous faces before him, "was it."

Standing quickly, he motioned us all to do likewise. The drill master was blunt in assisting those he felt were too slow in complying.

"To be a Ninja, one must have balance," said the chief instructor. "We will now determine who among you possess this skill, and to what degree. This will in large part determine the nature of the remainder of your training, so you are admonished to do your best. Follow me, and move quietly. Soon we will be in hostile territory."

We moved off in small groups and gradually strung out, obeying, without having to be told, the rule that forbids bunching up in enemy territory. We advanced safari style into the forest, following the chief instructor, with the drill instructor circling on both sides and behind like an outrider driving a stream of cattle.

We had come to a place where the stream widened to about fifteen feet, and here the chief instructor called a halt. We assembled under the cover of the foliage, to survey a fallen tree which bridged the water at a height of about eight feet.

"What is the best way to take a bridge?" The chief instructor nodded toward his associate, indicating that he should answer.

"Both ends at once!" the drill instructor replied, grinning.

"Take two men," suggested the chief instructor, pointing out two trainees near the front who had performed well during the march. The drill instructor and the two trainees disappeared into the forest.

No sign of the trio was seen or heard for some moments, giving those of us who remained hidden in the underbrush an opportunity to observe and rest. They soon reappeared ahead of us under the near embankment, downstream from the point of crossing. Each of them had removed his outer garments and boots and tied them into a tight bundle which was held high on one shoulder. One by one they slipped into the water, wading as far as possible, then swimming diagonally against the slow-moving current in a sort of modified sidestroke, which counteracted the flow of the stream, allowing them to cross directly to the other side (Figures 8, 9, 10). Once there, they quickly redressed and slithered into the cover of the trees beyond the bank. After a few suspenseful minutes the drill instructor strolled easily out onto the narrow log bridge and waved his arm to signal that it was safe to cross.

Figure 8. Silent river-crossing method with bundle. Secure the bundle on the shoulder and wade into the water, sliding feet forward for balance.

Figure 9. Bend the knees to lower yourself into the water.

Figure 10. Lower yourself further into the water until your lips are at water level, ready to duck under in case of attack. Swim forward using the sidestroke with the free hand.

Some members of the class must have wondered at the high-security precautions taken by the instructors, but if so none dared venture a question as we crept to the bridge. The chief instructor now appointed two men to serve as sentries, matching the pair on the yonder side, and motioned for the first student in line to mount the log. The student hesitated, as if unsure of his ability to negotiate the fallen tree trunk.

Urging him forward, the chief instructor posed with arms spread and rapidly walked as if on a tightrope to demonstrate the method that should be used to cross the log.

The first man crossed, followed by the rest of the group. As we advanced single file, the two students who had swum the river took up positions as flanking scouts, moving parallel to the main column. They vanished and came back into sight at intervals, as the brush thinned and then grew dense again. Our muffled breathing and occasional shuffling and crushing of leaves and twigs drew reproachful stares from the drill instructor. As we proceeded, the look in his eye grew increasingly menacing.

We traveled back downstream, toward the encampment. When we had progressed little more than a mile, the chief instructor raised his hand for a halt and called the group into a semicircle in front of him. As we knelt, the drill master stepped in front of us.

"You sound like a herd of swine!" he hissed. "If we were really in the jungle, every one of you would be dead! Listen: Do you hear any birds? Any game of any kind? If the enemy didn't find you and kill you, you would starve to death!" His fists tightened as if he dared us to disagree.

"Sensei is most correct," agreed the chief instructor. "From this point on we will observe absolute silence, moving as if by night, in total darkness."

We were directed to don blindfolds, link hands, and walk very slowly sideways in total silence while being lectured by the chief instructor on the various types of movement, or "steps."

"Movement at night must be made in absolute silence under the strictest discipline," he began. "Nocturnal infil-

tration of a combat zone or hostile territory is always dangerous, but more so if one is clumsy or ill-prepared. Avoid populated areas except when traveling under a *nom de voyage,*
or traveling name, with an appropriate cover identity. If possible, follow established game and animal trails when moving
through brush. Beware of ambush by enemy patrols and
sentries, who may be familiar with these pathways. Likewise, footpaths used by farmers and field workers should
be taken with care. Roads, paved or unpaved, are often well
traveled, and so provide a convenient place for you to stage
an ambush; but remember that they afford your enemy the
same advantage over you, should you frequent such routes!

"Familiarity with the terrain to be crossed is, of course,
a prerequisite for any mission. It is anticipated that the
agent in the field will carry whatever tools and devices he
thinks will be of value during the expedition.

"When traversing jungle terrain, move slowly and steadily,
pushing branches, creepers, and vines gently aside rather than
hacking your way through them. This is far quieter and will
leave less evidence of your passage. Learn to look ahead of
your next step, watching for openings and 'tunnels' through
the brush. When following animal trails, watch for snares and
traps. A stick or staff is useful for probing or clearing a path,
and is safer than the bare hand.

"Rugged and mountainous terrain, while easier to cross
without leaving a trail for the enemy to follow, has pitfalls
of its own for the traveler. Rock slides, steep treacherous
footing, and unforgiving stone make any crossing difficult.

"It is said that the Shaolin monks of ancient China had to
pass through a long tunnel filled with wooden dummies,
activated by various triggers and floorboards, which were
intended to strike and even kill the initiate. Only one trained
in the various disciplines of the temple could hope to successfully pass through the tunnel.

"So too, with the Ninja, who had not only to encounter
mechanical devices, but also traps, snares, and fellow agents
along a primitive combat course which was a large part of
their training and testing."

Blindfolded, walking sideways in a chain over the brushy,

uneven ground, we sounded more than ever like a herd of swine. Occasionally one of us stumbled, and the reaction could be felt up and down the line as the rest of us strove to maintain balance. The chief instructor, however, continued to lecture as if the situation were perfectly normal.

"The purpose of the Ninja combat course was to give the agent practical experience in quickly and quietly negotiating the various types of terrain encountered in the field. Each ryu, or style, emphasizes different techniques of silent movement and infiltration. The sensei, or teacher, should decide which obstacles should be constructed, and in what order they should be presented to the student. Obviously, the sensei must be familiar with each obstacle and the means for overcoming it, so that the proper technique may be practiced by the agent in training.

"Some rapid training courses are designed for a particular mission, being mock-ups or replicas of the site at which the task will be executed. This method permits quick assimilation of the details of the mission, but relies on the inherent ability and ingenuity of the agent to adapt to any discrepancy which may occur due to misinformation or miscalculation. Ideally, the course which offers the greatest variety of opportunity for experience under day, night, and foul-weather conditions over an extended period is preferred. Under any conditions, speed and stealth are the hallmarks of ninjitsu.

"A third commonly encountered hazard was the wet crossing. A mud trap, for example, produces a squishy, sucking sound when crossed. Mud can be safely negotiated by sliding the feet as much as possible. This method is also effective in ankle-deep water, as well as in the rice-paddy trap—knee-deep holes designed to twist the leg, sometimes filled with stakes—as it allows the Ninja to feel his way among unseen obstacles. Move slowly to avoid sloshing the water about.

"Falling at night," continued the chief instructor, as a trainee tripped over what sounded like a dead tree limb, "is noisy and may attract enemy fire. Most falls are caused by stumbling. Therefore, the less one trips or stumbles, the more quietly he will move. In a wet crossing involving knee-deep water or snow, lift the foot higher and point the toes downward when stepping.

"The logical follow-up to the wet-crossing hazard is a carefully manicured area intended to mark the passage of an intruder. You can rub out your tracks behind you. By using the cross step, you will confuse the enemy as to your direction of travel, since any footprint you may inadvertently leave will point about ninety degrees away from the direction in which you are traveling. Unusual and misleading tracks may be left by leaping, taking extremely long steps, or hand-springing.

"Grass covered with a light frost, morning dew, and fresh snow can be deadly accurate in recording your progress. Also dangerous are a sandy beach and a dusty road after a light rain.

"In olden times, any of the hazard areas that I have just described might have been strewn with trip wires, snares, and all manner of other devices intended to slow one's progress or inflict injury. And, from time to time, the Ninja trainee was certain to encounter a spear or club launched from a place of concealment, sometimes followed by the wielder or the sensei himself.

"The classical Ninja combat course always began in a stand of bamboo. Since the *heng pu,* or cross step, was the foundation of the art, it was the first test of the student's ability [Figures 11, 12, 13]. Initiates were required to follow a thread through the upright bamboo canes in a specific amount of time. The only quick way to accomplish this was to move sideways instead of straight ahead, quickly adjusting one's height to the openings and passageways which presented themselves in the maze. Any one of several types of hazard would then confront him.

"One such hazard was typically a stretch of gravel pathway. Early Ninja discovered that the ornamental stone walkways which surrounded many an ornate dwelling actually served as burglar alarms. The grinding of the rocks against one another produced a characteristic sound which would alert guards or sentries.

"Two methods of crossing gravel were commonly taught.

Figure 11. Ninja cross step. Preparatory stance.

Figure 12. Cross step in front.

Figure 13. Cross step behind.

In one, the belt, or *obi,* was rolled across the rock. By treading on this, the Ninja muffled his footsteps. The other method was to slowly place the edge of the foot, then the ball, and last the heel on the gravel with each step. It will be noted by the observant that this pattern of weight shift and distribution is precisely the same as that of the basic cross step.

"Another hazard of the combat course was dry leaves and twigs. For this, the *p'a pu,* or night walking step, was used. Extending the arms for balance, the Ninja would stand on one leg and clear a spot for the next step with the toes of the other foot. Progress is slow, but quiet.

"The *she pu,* or serpent step, is practiced when negotiating grass. When the grass is high, it provides good cover. Care must be taken to move with the waving of the grass when the wind causes it to sway. Crawling through furrows or ditches is another way to cross cleared fields. Open spaces may be quickly crossed by rushing from one point of concealment to another in a low crouching posture. When traversing a very large area, run in a serpentine pattern and drop unexpectedly to the ground from time to time. By this method, fields of fire may sometimes be successfully passed.

"Stone walls, chain-link fence, barbed wire, barricaded logs, inclined walls, a cliff face, and trees provide cover and concealment but can also act as barriers. Any competent program training for stealth and speed should teach how to overcome such obstacles by ducking behind cover, rolling forward or to the side out of sight, stopping suddenly, and changing direction, as well as climbing, swinging, and balancing.

"In an aerial crossing one travels a single line between two points, either walking slack-wire style, hand over hand, with knees hooked underneath, or sliding along the top of the wire or rope. Well-established trails may be equipped with a commando line, which is actually two ropes, one above the other. The top rope is held for balance. The rope bridge is similar, with one line for walking and one at waist level on either side. Walking the balance beam is good practice to prepare the Ninja for operating among rooftops.

"Of course," the chief instructor continued, "that which

ascends must eventually descend. Two methods were generally taught, rappeling and sliding. This area would also include high diving and *ukemi,* the art of feather falling. Ninja were adept at this, having found that with proper training they could virtually drop from one handhold to another down an almost sheer surface and land with a roll or tumble to dissipate the impact, much as modern paratroopers do.

"Rappeling is essentially the art of sliding vertically down a rope without burning the hands. It is extremely dangerous, and requires supervised instruction. Likewise, the customary 'slide for life' ride down an incline line to a sudden drop in a river, which is used by most infantry installations in the United States, requires facilities and either a pulley handgrip arrangement or leather sleeve for the rider. Such training reduces or eliminates fear of heights. The traditional Ninja exercise of prolonged hanging by the arms to develop courage is the preliminary exercise for this stage.

"Fire crossing was designed to instill courage in the potential agent. First was the barefoot fire walk, and second the fire pit, which had to be jumped as flames leaped to engulf the student.

"In the arcane, or mystery, schools, initiates were also taught to walk on broken glass and climb the ladder of swords as tests of ability, but such training does not properly fall into the study of survival skills. Nevertheless, like the rice-paper test of the monks, in which the student attempted to walk on a length of the fragile material without tearing it, practicing for such tests developed the same abilities and illustrated the same principles of movement as did the combat course. These abilities, once acquired, are useful in many fields of endeavor, from hunting to escape and evasion.

"The objectives of this training, then, are basically to learn to move quietly and disturb little. This is the way of Nature; and the secret of practicing it is balance. In the martial arts application of the *kuji ashi,* or silent steps, it is said 'The waist is the banner, and goes into battle first.' This means that when one moves, the hips should lead the action. Keep the body centered above the soles of the feet, holding the shoulders square and level.

"Every man has the ability to develop these skills. Isolated in hostile or contested territory, cut off from civilization by disaster or design, most human beings quickly learn, some say remember, how to stalk and overcome wild game with ingenuity. In modern life, these lessons benefit us by enabling us to maintain a calm and balanced disposition in the face of frustration and adversity."

We had traveled blindly for perhaps a mile, perhaps further; it was difficult to tell. The chief instructor now lapsed into silence, and I found that we had become quiet enough to listen to the sigh of the wind in the trees and the chirping of insects and birds. We had discovered that we could look down the sides of our noses and watch our feet. This held our attention and soon led to our stepping in each other's footsteps, disguising the size of the party. Since at first this required walking at a snail's pace, deeply bending the knees for the cross-stepping, it was extremely tiring even for the well conditioned.

A secondary effect was confusion, and this was doubtless the intent of the masters. By the time we arrived at our destination, few of us had any idea in which direction we had been traveling, or for how long, although the sun held about three o'clock.

We were permitted to stop and remove the blindfolds. Our eyes slowly readjusted to the brilliant sunlight. We maintained our silence, nursing sore and aching muscles, or gently rubbing our eyes.

"You may speak now," said the chief instructor, allowing us a few moments of conversation among ourselves before continuing with his lecture.

"You have learned a new way of walking silently, the hunting step," he resumed at length, "and you have learned to work together as a single serpent to move in total darkness. The Mandarin Chinese have a term for this type of movement. It is called *gong he*, or working together. But a human chain, like any other kind of chain, is only as strong as its weakest link. Therefore, we strive to make each man as strong as possible by having him master the proper walking techniques."

CONCEALMENT

"You have learned the art of not being heard, of stealthily moving over the earth with the cross step. Now we must address the question of not being seen. In ancient times the techniques of cover, camouflage, and concealment were known as *inpo,* the art of hiding.

"For those of you unfamiliar with covert operations, let me explain that this training is solely for tactical purposes. You are being taught to serve as an armed body in support of a field agent; every finger is a dagger, every hand a sword, every man an army.

"Basically, you will surreptitiously follow the agent in and out during the performance of his mission, and make your presence known only if called upon by secret signal. Your assignment is to act as backup; there may be only one of you dispatched, or there may be many, each unaware of the others unless they are called out of hiding by the agent. Often, the agent himself will be unaware of these secondary forces sent to ensure that the mission will be completed. Thus, if one were a double agent, he might report to the enemy instead of performing the duty he was sent out to perform. In this event, the shadow Ninja would be obliged to kill him and complete the task.

"From now on, when I clap my hands together, you will turn and run for cover. There you will hide, following me unseen, until I snap my fingers; then you will run forward and kneel beside me at the ready.

"The military definition of *undercover* is 'out of enemy sight and line of fire'; *concealment* is the state of being out of sight but vulnerable to enemy fire; and *camouflage* is the art of blending in with one's surroundings so that, while you may technically be "in sight," you are not seen and therefore are not vulnerable. All are aspects of the art of invisibility—ninjitsu!

"Each of you wears a coverall garment issued to you at the time of your arrival. It is of a color and nature to blend with the terrain and is therefore considered camouflage. If you will look in your left side vest pocket, you will find a soft mask designed to cover your entire head and face, except for the eyes, to prevent your skin from reflecting light and thus revealing your position at night. This is simpler than using paint or burnt cork, and provides some protection from insects as well. Furthermore, in cities and congested places, the mask is quickly removed and discarded, causing the Ninja agent to "disappear," while a normal looking person takes his place. Get rid of the mask, and you get rid of the evidence, making identification more difficult.

"There is no talking while wearing the mask. Each agent works entirely alone, independent of all the others, yet the efforts of all harmonize to complete the mission. Because there is little, if any, communication between agents during an operation, ninjitsu is sometimes called the 'silent way.'"

Clap! The chief instructor's cupped palms came together in a sudden flash of motion which resounded like thunder. We were shocked by the unexpectedness of the gesture, and also by its resonance and resounding echo. Then, as quickly as if we had rehearsed the maneuver, we spread out from him in all directions, dissipating in an instant toward the perimeter like a cloud of smoke.

Some, lacking skill in hiding, selected the most obvious places. But others, more experienced, took advantage of shallow depressions in the surface of the ground, and of the knee-high dry grass which filled the clearing. Thus, they were able to hide very close to the chief instructor and save themselves a good deal of running back and forth during the ensuing drill.

For over two hours we played an elaborate game of hide-and-seek, with students scrambling to kneel around the chief instructor, and just as swiftly duck for cover. The drill instructor, of course, followed anyone and everyone, ferreting out even the most cunning and inflicting his own brand of verbal and physical discipline before demonstrating the proper method of using whatever cover had been selected.

I soon discovered that it was necessary to watch the chief intently from my place of concealment in order to see the signal to assemble. Certainly I could not hear it, since the sound carried no more than a few feet at best. It was also necessary to listen just as intently for any sound of the approaching drill instructor. Within the short time period, most had mastered the needed acumen and performed the exercise quickly and with precision.

It must be said that the leader, while keeping the rhythm irregular enough to prevent boredom, never took advantage of his position of nonmovement. He did not sit nor pace about restlessly. Instead, his movements were purposeful and direct. Several times he pointed out where a student could be seen from his vantage point, permitting the student to adjust his position to ensure invisibility. When all seemed to have grasped the principle, and their second wind, he began to slowly walk toward the north.

The game continued as he made his way back through the forest along the narrow trail. Now, instead of a single file of recruits flanked by two outriders, there strode a single samurai, virtually surrounded by a legion of camouflaged and unseen soldiers of the night. Little wonder he could walk with confidence. So well had the students learned, birds chirped and bees hummed undisturbed by our passing.

It was dusk when we topped a little knoll and found ourselves just behind a stand of hardwoods. As the sun set, its red glow kindled the tips of the pines, and the western sky was ablaze with color; yet already the air had begun to cool. Already night let its icy fingers pull the shadows of the woods closer and deeper about the group, scattered as we were on and around the trail.

Once again he called us together and gave the word to relax when we had formed as required.

"Hoods off," he whispered, and we replaced them in our left side vest pockets. Breathing more easily, we looked expectantly toward the chief instructor, some doubtless hardly realizing the time of day or that the practice session was over, so great was their fatigue and exhaustion.

"You have done well," he began softly. "We have worked very hard this day, and had no lunch to boot. In the morning we ran to the south; we ran for a long time and covered a lot of ground. All day we have been zigzagging east and north, back toward the main camp." He smiled. "I said earlier that we would be hunting all day for dinner. Now is the time for that meal. From this point on, you will be on your own. I will only say that the lodge is due north of this clearing. It will be up to each of you to find your way there, for supper, by means of the art of navigation."

NAVIGATION

"In olden days," the chief instructor continued, "the Chinese developed a primitive compass consisting of a magnetized needle floating on the surface tension of a bowl of shallow water. By far the most ancient method of orienting oneself, however, is to navigate by the stars.

"From our earthly viewpoint, the largest star appears to be the sun, a fiery ball of exploding gases which rises in the east and sets in the west. Finding directional north during daylight hours is easily accomplished by rising early and facing the sun as it breaks over the horizon. You will be looking east. During winter in the Northern Hemisphere, the sun will be somewhat south of due east. Turn so the right shoulder faces the sun. You are now facing north. In the afternoon, aim the left shoulder at the setting sun, which will be west as you look north. Select a landmark directly ahead; this may be a high peak of a mountain, or a point on the horizon. This will be the cardinal point of your imaginary compass. Next, determine the direction in which you wish to travel and choose a landmark. Move toward the selected point at the proper pace.

"A similar trick may be used when hunting in unfamiliar territory. Pick out the tallest tree in the vicinity and keep it always to one side or the other. In this way you may circle-search the area without losing your sense of direction or becoming disoriented.

"Follow the natural lay of the land, always keeping an eye on a pylon guidepost if one is in sight. Much unexplored territory was opened up by pioneers who followed rivers and streams. Often these provide an alternative means of transportation and supply of food, but their meandering path, while taking the course of least resistance, may be long and tortuous, and not necessarily the shortest route in your direction.

"In mountainous or foothill country, avoid silhouetting yourself against the skyline, but travel the ridges and slopes. This high ground offers many good vantage points. The valleys provide cover and concealment, but may impede your progress with thick undergrowth or bush.

"At night, directional orientation is even more critical. Great care must be taken in determining direction at night, since often even a slight error is not easily discovered until it is too late.

"The most reliable method, in the Northern Hemisphere, is by locating the North Star, also known as Polaris, or the polestar. At the North Pole, this celestial spark is theoretically directly overhead. Certainly, in the arctic, the angle above the observer is so great that it is useless as a landmark. North of the equator, however, it is clearly visible as the brightest star in the heavens. The closer to the equator, the nearer the horizon the star will be. At the equator, it is too low to be seen.

"Polaris is at the end of the handle of the constellation known as the Little Dipper. The companion constellation known as the Big Dipper will be to the left, and the Chair of Cassiopeia, a cluster of five large stars, to the right.

"Look directly down from the polestar and site a landmark to determine true north. Select the direction in which you wish to travel and move off [Figure 14].

"Ancient Ninja were exceedingly familiar with the night sky and, in some cases, rivaled the knowledge of the astronomers of the period."

The crisp, cool night air stirred around us, and the flickering stars winked and twinkled in the cloudless sky, dimly lighting the gathering as the speaker finished.

Clap! Again the command to vanish. This we did, automatically now and in most dramatic fashion. When the dust had cleared, I looked for the chief instructor, awaiting his signal to reappear, even though it was not likely I could have seen or heard him snap his fingers.

But he too had gone, vanished like his followers, and the

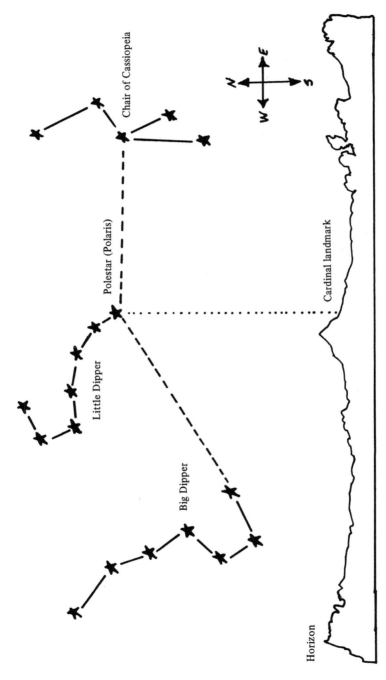

Figure 14. Diagram for siting the North Star (Polaris).

drill instructor, who had quietly slipped away during the lecture, was nowhere to be seen either. Due to the very nature of the drill, there were no longer any comrades to be called upon for assistance. Each of us was on his own in unfamiliar territory, with only his wits to enable him to survive.

We made our way silently through the trees and underbrush; had I not known better, I would have thought myself to be the only human in the forest. By following the directions of the chief instructor, I soon found myself on a shallow incline on the far side of the wood. One more barrier of shrubs and brush, and I could see the glowing yellow light of the bunkhouse porch below the beacon of the guiding star.

Some inner voice must have held us all in the perimeter cover around the building, as if all day with no lunch had somehow conditioned us for this moment. After a while, when he had allowed sufficient time for even the slowest to find his way home, the chief instructor appeared on the porch and snapped his fingers, and would-be Ninja warriors immediately began to materialize from the bushes. All enjoyed a hearty meal that evening.

TRAINING HALL

After dinner, there was a short period during which the members of the training team were allowed to freshen up and relax for a few moments. This permitted the more spiritual of the group to admire the night sky, breathing slowly and deeply as we stood about or perched on the various stools and railings on the porch. The Oriental girl whom I had admired earlier wandered out to the porch and seated herself on one of the railings. She introduced herself as Lee. We exchanged a few pleasantries and then fell silent, appreciating the beauty of the evening. Some sat inside, enjoying a cigarette or finishing a cup of coffee, joking, and pretending to complain about the food. The sounds of conversation and laughter drifted out onto the porch, accentuating, rather than disturbing, my sense of well-being.

Just when it seemed that we might begin either to doze off or become involved in some secondary activity, the drill instructor came in and conducted the entire company to a large barn on the property which had been converted into a combination gymnasium and dojo.

When we had first entered the training camp, before the welcoming speech of the chief instructor, certain landmarks had been pointed out to us by one of the advanced students as being of historical or topographical importance. The drill instructor now reminded us of these landmarks and instructed us regarding the proper sequence in which they were to be related to when we returned from the field. The particular order we followed in relation to them would indicate to which team or group we belonged, even though no open sign of recognition would be given or expected. If the entering party did not follow this procedure, he or she would be marked as an outsider, or the others might assume that a Ninja guide was leading the party under duress.

A similar recognition procedure, the drill instructor explained, was employed upon entering the meditation hall. Each member of the class was expected to bow at the door to demonstrate respect for the ancient teachers, whose likenesses hung above the portal. Persons not performing this small ritual, once inside, were open to attack by the "little man above the door," actually a sentry, posted before class, who was skilled in combat techniques in and around doorways.

Once one was safely inside, a second bow was required at the edge of the tatamied floor, and shoes or sandals were removed. Had any of the party been armed, it was explained, they would have been expected to place their weapons in one of the racks to the right side of the large doors. If one were a traveler, any gear or baggage would be placed to the left of the entryway. Following these customs would signify the peaceful intent of the visitor. A second sentry was usually present in ninjitsu schools hidden beneath a trapdoor at the edge of the mat. He would be assigned to trip and throw any intruder from this place of concealment, enabling the "thumb," or head student, to pin the intruder instantly, and thus forestall an attack on the sensei. Furthermore, other sentries could be posted in the rafters and behind obstacles, each practicing inpo. When these ceremonies were initiated, we were told, the stakes were life and death.

The bow is a courtesy which is rendered to those of superior position or rank, the drill instructor continued. The salutation is not merely an ordinary form of greeting, but also an expression of respect for one's opponent or instructor. It should be made seriously before and after exercises and sparring since these are contests in which we express both state of mind and control.

In addition to the commonly seen bow of many Oriental cultures, both the Ninja and their brothers of the underworld, the Yakuza, practice with an ancient type of bow which is used to introduce oneself for an audience with an *oyabun,* or head man, or when confronting an unfamiliar agent. Since it is not an obvious gesture of salutation, it often passes unnoticed except to those who know it.

The drill instructor proceeded to demonstrate the bow (Figure 15). "From the position of military attention, take one full step to the rear with the left foot and shift your weight back over that leg so that the right leg may be essentially straight without locking the knee. Hold out the left hand palm down and extend the right hand out in front palm up as if asking for a bowl of rice. Look down rather than at the individual you mean to address, and pause. If he too is an agent, he will respond with the same or similar gesture. At a sign from the ranking member on the scene, you may speak.

"Begin by saying, 'Please allow me to present my credentials.' If you carry a message or document, profer it then in the right hand. Identify yourself by name, rank, and clan, and briefly state your business."

The sensei was a smallish man with round eyeglasses and an Oriental appearance, although his English was unaccented. In a deep, resonant voice, he asked the class to be seated in a comfortable cross-legged position.

"We," he waved an arm behind him to indicate two advanced students dressed in black gis, "would like to take this opportunity to welcome each of you to the fascinating world of espionage. We are eager to assist you in your study

Figure 15. The Yakuza bow.

and help you develop a strong and successful attitude so that you may achieve the goals you desire.

"There are many things which the novice must learn in addition to the techniques of our martial art. First, let me assure you that the ideas and principles of practice and study handed down from master to student over the generations, which we will share with you in class, are proven methods of building a sound mind in a sound body. They will enable you to advance quickly and efficiently from being a good soldier to a good spy. Let me urge you to take advantage of these guidelines, which have been tried and true through the centuries.

"Second, the dojo, or training hall, is a place of culture. Therefore compose yourself and behave seriously without talking idly or acting noisily. Both during practice and during matches, one must maintain good deportment and be attentive to others, who are also trying to learn lessons in self-improvement.

"Ninjitsu is a very personal field of study. We have no quotas or mandatory requirements. We, your instructors, take a genuine interest in your continued growth and development; but the ultimate success or failure of your ambition will depend on you. We require no major investments, no previous experience, and no special educational background. Our teachings are the property of all and belong to everyone. You must decide how much time per week you will devote to the practice and study of what you will learn here. Practice is the key to the mastery of any subject, self-discipline is the key to practice. Every hour spent in study, experimentation, and drill will be repaid in skill, confidence, health, and vitality. Make a commitment to yourself and formulate your future goals and objectives. The amount of time and effort you spend is not nearly as important as the attitude with which you begin. Prepare yourself now.

"If one wishes to obtain the best result from the workout, one must consistently observe moderation in eating, drinking, and sleeping. One must also, as a matter of course, refrain from eating and drinking water during practice as well as immediately before or after the exercises. One must keep the body clean and the nails neatly trimmed, since minor scratches may result in infections if untreated. During the exercises, one should close the mouth and breathe through the nose. To engage in *kumite,* or sparring, *randori,* or free-throwing practice, and weapons practice, you must have the permission and supervision of the instructors.

"These rules and bylaws are for the protection of the dojo and its membership. Those who do not conform to them may be expelled by the governing board at any time. I must be notified immediately of any injury you sustain so that proper first aid may be applied. Techniques not taught in class may not be used during practice. This must be strictly enforced. The dojo is not a place for horseplay or vulgar language. Proper etiquette must be maintained at all times.

"Finally, cooperation should be the ruling spirit of the training hall, since it is the common house of all who study here.

"Karate is the art of defending oneself against armed attackers without the use of weapons. A pistol, club, or knife may well be an advantage, but may not always be within easy reach, whereas the hands and feet of a trained martial artist can be considered deadly weapons.

"Ninjitsu, on the other hand, is the art of the invisible assassin. You have begun practicing the skills of inpo, which relate to hiding and penetrating enemy lines unseen. Now we will take up *tonpo,* those techniques which relate to escaping from enemy territory or custody.

"The first thing one must learn in this regard is ukemi, or how to fall safely."

Ninja Side Roll

"Many skilled martial artists can identify an opponent by the stance he assumes at the beginning of combat. This is a function of years of observation and practice. But, if there is such a thing as a hallmark of ninjitsu, by which practitioners can be readily identified, it is the side roll," continued the sensei.

"The purpose of this technique is to quickly vanish in order to avoid any potentially life-threatening situation. This is the most fundamental part of ukemi, the art of falling safely.

"Begin in a wide stance, with arms apart, presenting as large a figure as possible. This is an old judo trick to psychologically intimidate the opponent by making him think you are larger than you actually are.

"Immediately as he makes his approach, snap your feet together, pull in your arms, tuck your head, and drop as quickly as possible into a tight ball. This presents a very small target to the opponent, and, if the timing is right, he will lose sight of you for a second.

"Without pausing, push off strongly with one foot and roll swiftly along the back and shoulders while staying as tightly curled as you can. At night, or in semidarkness, any rustling or noise made by this action helps to confuse the opponent as you roll out of danger.

"Startle the enemy by regaining your feet in a wide stance [Figures 16, 17, 18, 19, 20]. The effect is that of vanishing and reappearing elsewhere."

Figure 16. Ninja side roll. Begin in a wide stance.

Figure 17. Drop into a tight ball as quickly as possible.

Figure 18. Roll sideways on the knees, elbows, shoulders, and hips.

Figure 19. Complete the roll by coming to the hands and knees.

Figure 20. Push up and use the momentum of the roll to bring you erect.

Ninja Back Roll

"The next logical step in the art of falling," sensei instructed, "is the back roll, an auxiliary movement to the side roll. It is based on the principle of yielding. If the opponent is determined to enter a given space, the Ninja, having no claim on that space, will often give it to him rather than contend for that which is not his. Furthermore, it is a second

Figure 21. Ninja back roll. Begin in the hands-up stance.

method of absenting oneself from the area of potential danger by placing a greater distance between the combatants.

"From the hands-up position, again quickly snap the legs together and fold the arms over the knees, dropping into a compact ball below knee level.

"Without stopping, fall backward, throwing the hands back over the head to lift the shoulders and allow the head to clear without twisting the neck. Lift and throw the feet back, up, and over.

"As the feet land, use the arms to lift the upper body off the ground, and allow your momentum to carry you to your feet once again in a wide stance with arms raised [Figures 21, 22, 23, 24].

"The back roll is also effective against a straight-arm push against the chest, or any time when one must retreat backward to avoid being struck."

Figure 22. Kneel and fall back.

Figure 23. Roll backward in a tight ball.

Figure 24. Stand erect.

Ninja Forward Roll

"The opposite of the previous technique, used to gain ground toward an opponent, is the forward roll. When fighting, it is sometimes advisable to attack suddenly. By this method, one may often quickly bridge the gap between the combatants and in relative safety. Likewise, the unexpected

Figure 25. Ninja forward roll. Begin in the hands-up stance.

rush forward, and sudden appearance on top of the enemy, may stun him long enough to provide the advantage of surprise necessary to prevail.

"Once again, from the hands-up position, drop quickly into a tight ball. Push off strongly with both legs as you roll forward, using the hands and arms to protect the head while rolling.

"As the feet come over, roll smoothly onto the hips. Do not bang down; this is a circular motion designed to dissipate the impact of falling evenly over the intervening space. Be ready to kick out to defend yourself if necessary, and keep the arms across the chest defensively as well. Let your momentum carry you forward and back to your feet (Figures 25, 26, 27, 28).

"With a minimum of practice, one can learn the proper range for this and the other associated techniques. They are the foundation of the art of invisibility, just as is the heng pu, or cross step.

"Advanced techniques include cartwheel kicks, handspring double heel kicks (scorpion style), jumping attacks (flying side kicks), and low sweeping kicks."

Figure 26. Kneel down and drop forward.

Figure 27. Roll forward.

Figure 28. Stand erect.

Meditation

The class ended with a short period of meditation. Sensei had us sit cross-legged on the floor, hands in laps, thumbs touching. He then instructed us in what he called the proper manner of breathing, as follows.

"With eyes closed, inhale deeply and fully without strain, allowing the shoulders to rise as the chest expands, and draw the air into the hara, or center, a point two inches below the navel. Exhale, without being forceful, and expel the air which was exchanged in the lungs for the fresh air, holding the *chi,* or vital energy, in the abdomen. Inhale again, moving the chi, which was warmed and heated in the abdomen, to the base of the spine, as the new breath enters. Exhale as before. Now there is one breath in the hara, and one at the base of the spine. Touch the tip of the tongue to the center of the palate, not too far back, and inhale a third time, tightening the buttock muscles and drawing the chi up the spine, over the head, and to the tip of the nose. Exhale as before, allowing the hara to relax each time before tightening the abdomen and raising the energy upward. One may feel minor blockage between the shoulder blades at first, or tingling of the scalp. Do not let the energy accumulate in the skull, as this will cause headaches. Repeat the cycle from tip of nose to tip of nose nine times. This is one repetition. Do nine repetitions."

We all remarked on how much better we felt afterward, relaxed, yet fresh and alert. To relieve any muscle tension that remained, sensei had us massage the *san ri* point on our upper shins to promote circulation.

As part of the meditation exercise, the class was instructed in the art of haiku, or "black poems." These are composed of three lines of five, seven, and five syllables. Each student composes his own, and it becomes a private mantra, or verse by which to live.

"The haiku practice derives from the ancient samurai technique of calming the mind before a major battle, or when facing imminent death," the sensei explained. "By concentrating on the structure, which some find most confining and others maintain encompasses all that need be said on the subject, one is able to quiet one's jangled nerves and view a crisis dispassionately. Warriors in the service of the emperor were almost always at peril, and were often sent out to certain death, so too, the Ninja, operating without support behind enemy lines. Thus, the exercise was of enormous benefit for sustaining a dwindling spirit.

"It was the practice of ancient Ninja to meditate alone prior to undertaking an assignment, especially a particularly dangerous or difficult one, in order to purify the mind and body and mentally prepare for the task ahead. During these sessions, an agent sometimes experienced a transcendental state of awareness which occasionally permitted him to catch a glimpse of the future, a premonition of what was to come. Based upon this experience, he would compose a haiku and pledge himself to the mission."

Class ended with a formal bow to the sensei, and we were led back to the bunkhouse along the beaten path that wound from the barn back to the house. There was little talking, since most of us were bone-tired from the long day's exertion. Despite the massage, my legs still ached from the morning's run.

One by one we finished brushing our teeth and preparing for bed. At last, the final three struggled to their cots, just after the light had been turned off by one of the drill instructor's assistants. Within a few moments the sound of snoring drifted across the room. The crickets chirped, their music gradually dwindling as they too settled down for the evening. Outside the window clouds skated across the moon, borne on the chill night air high above the treetops. Solitary owls hooted as they hunted on the wings of darkness.

Inside the bunkhouse the wooden floor made occasional popping and creaking sounds due to the change in temperature from day to night, but generally, stillness reigned. Soon I too fell asleep.

It was perhaps an hour after the assistant had turned off the light when I woke, wondering whether I had dreamed the sound of the chief instructor's hands clapping softly together. I was dully considering whether to thoroughly rouse myself or succumb once more to the temptation of sleep, when suddenly the room was filled with light. The harsh glare of what appeared to be high-intensity flashlight beams were shining directly into my face. I was roughly shaken and hauled out of bed, and I heard the others being herded, as I was, into the living room. As my eyes adjusted to the sudden brightness, I saw that our assailants were men in uniform, badges dangling from their belts and jackets. Pistols and nightsticks hovered menacingly over the members of our group, who stood about half-dressed, looking confused and disoriented.

Flashlight beams now focused on one of the two advanced students who had taken part in the river crossing earlier that day.

"Who are you?" a voice demanded out of the darkness.

The student made no reply, but swallowed visibly.

A disembodied fist flashed out of the gloom and slammed into the side of the young man's head, knocking him into a kneeling position on the floor. Instinctively, he put his hand up to cover the injury as he staggered to a chair.

"I said, what's your name?" came the voice of the invisible interrogator once again.

As before, there was no reply; the victim rubbed the side of his head tenderly.

A hand snaked forward, seized him by the hair, and roughly jerked him to his feet. He was dragged outside. The silence in the room grew oppressive, although no more than a minute or two could have passed before it was shattered by the sound of a single shot.

Silence again, as the echoes of the gunshot died away in the night; and then came the sound of the interrogator's boots mounting the two wooden steps onto the porch. I thought the pounding of my heart must be audible to everyone in the room. As we stood corralled inside the circle of lights, awaiting the interrogator's return, the fear in the room was palpable; you could smell it in the air. The screen door creaked on its hinges and banged shut on the heels of the murderer.

There was a soft click as the lights were turned on, and soon details of the living room could be seen once more. We were surrounded by a ring of flashlights, set upon various ledges and shelves about the room. The drill instructor's two assistants were lounging casually against the bookcase. One of them, the student whom I had supposed was just beaten and killed, was smiling, obviously alive and well.

"You are all dead!" screamed the drill master. "Every one of you would have been captured and taken to prison, if not simply executed. You must observe security at all times. *At all times!"*

"Quite so," agreed the chief instructor, from his position by the door. "If you were in hostile territory, your position could easily have been compromised by agents within your own group." He smiled.

"These two men," he said, waving toward his "victim" and the other assistant, the two trainees who had swum the river, "are advanced students, planted in your midst as part of *their* training."

CAPTURE AND INTERROGATION

"The possibility of capture and interrogation is always present," the drill instructor went on. "No one knows how he will endure a specific situation until it occurs; but we do know that eventually all things must end.

"Many secret agents prefer death to capture and torture by hostile agencies. A self-imposed death was called *seppuku* or *hara-kiri,* meaning belly cut, by the Japanese genin, or field agent. Ancient Ninja usually stabbed themselves in the throat or bit off their tongues, either of which would indicate that the secret information had not been disclosed.

"Modern spies also follow this tradition. Some pilots on secret missions are equipped with cyanide capsules or small cyanide needles with which to inject themselves on point of capture to prevent compromise of classified information to which they are privy.

"Clandestine operatives may also have a hollow tooth fitted with a safety cap and filled with a toxin that causes instant death. Still another variation is the poisoned thumbnail, which is chewed, apparently involuntarily.

"The ancient Chinese and Japanese, among others, were

masters of interrogation by torture. The human body can take only a certain amount of pain before the brain 'turns itself off,' rendering the individual unconscious. After continuous torture, the body becomes essentially numb to pain. Some yogis can mentally slow their heart rate or make themselves impervious to needles piercing their skin. But even these feats require energy; eventually the body dies.

"There are, of course, many effective psychological methods available to the interrogator. Flashing or extremely bright lights, like those we used tonight, sudden loud noises, like horn or whistle blasts, or even the total silence of solitary confinement, are at his disposal. An interrogator may also use mind-altering drugs. When a victim is sufficiently disoriented, pain may be his only contact with reality.

"By inducing confusion and disorientation, the interrogator breaks down his victim's will. Of course, physical pain, prolonged immobility, and verbal intimidation are effective and proven techniques. Suspense, or the anticipation of pain, is an important factor in torture. Macabre games of chance, like Russian Roulette, in which the stakes are life and death, entail both fascination and terror.

"Before interrogation, the captured agent is rendered helpless, since otherwise he may wreak great destruction and possibly escape. Rendering the victim immobile is sometimes accomplished by threat of weaponry and sometimes by physical restraints, but in either event, the subject will be forced to look up at his interrogator. This is psychologically defeating.

"The interrogator will then identify himself and make assurances that he can and will obtain results, and is, in fact, eager to employ the full weight and authority of his position to do so. If you are captured, therefore, it is in your best interests to make this interview as short and truthful as he requires. Some sign of understanding from you is obligatory at this stage. Your response will be interpreted as either acceptance or challenge.

"He will then pose the question. It may be simple, like name, rank, and serial number, or complex, like the position of your unit and its mission and composition.

"No matter what you answer, you will not be believed until your story is confirmed, either by another source, or by your protestations of truthfulness up to the point of death.

"Those for whom capture and torture are occupational hazards must consider methods of escape from such situations. Seppuku was considered an honorable way to conclude a mission in ancient Japan, as it obviated any possibility that an agent might talk under pressure. In the event that seppuku seems impossible, undesirable, or too extreme as an initial measure, you should know other means of getting out of a tight situation.

"Few restraints were designed to hold a person forever. With enough effort over a long enough period of time, one can almost certainly work free of ropes, even if they are tied around your chest, waist, and ankles. A standard magician's escape from 100 feet of rope on stage relies heavily on the fact that several volunteers working with one piece of line will often impede each other and work at cross purposes. So too with a single individual. The longer it takes to tie someone up, the more bored one becomes, with the result that the last knots are looser than the first and the rope is wrapped more. All of this contributes to slack in the line, which enables one to work free. In the interests of time, free the hands first. A small knife, thumbnail-size razor blade, or broken piece of glass can often sever the necessary cords, but usually one must rely on fingers and practice.

"It is essential, if you entertain any thoughts of escaping, that you implement them as soon as possible after capture. The longer you remain in captivity, the more brainwashed you are likely to become, and the less likely you are to carry out a successful escape attempt.

"The farther you are inside enemy-held territory, the more difficult and arduous will be your journey back to friendly areas. During that trek, everything you see and hear will be of tremendous importance. A small detail may save your life. It is said in espionage that the tiniest thing may take on the greatest significance; and in ninjitsu it is taught that not a feather may be added or an ounce lost in order to maintain proper balance. Each facet of terrain and checkpoint, as well as intelligence considerations like size, strength, and location of enemy forces are critical at such times.

"Tomorrow each of you will be questioned regarding your recollection of the night's events. It will be a test of your powers of observation and recall. Remember, incidents run together, details blur. Different people view different aspects of an event and place importance on different parts. All accounts are hearsay at best, and the telling of a tale only serves to increase its proportions. So do not gossip among yourselves, since this may lead to distortion of the facts. Do not believe rumors, but wait for confirmation of your report."

Humbly digesting this revelation, we returned at last to bed.

The next day, each student was quietly taken aside and debriefed by the chief instructor. It was explained to us at that time that the body may sleep, but the mind never, meaning that even when one is asleep, the senses continue to take in and process information on a subconscious level. With careful coaching and elicitation of information by the questioner, many hitherto unremembered details of the events were pointed out. The dangers of cooperating with the interrogation were made obvious when certain details which had not occurred were suggested.

If the subject agreed that they happened, it indicated an eagerness to please or lack of confidence which might be exploited in an unsuspecting witness. This, of course, was unacceptable, since it is the memory of the agent, his ability to remember and transmit military and strategic information that makes one an asset to the intelligence community.

When asked for a description of the injury suffered by the person supposedly questioned and killed, for example, some reported a bruise, some made mistakes in the number and nature of the blows, some saw blood. Yet in reality no injury had occurred. The chief instructor had not actually struck the student at all! The latter had merely covered his cheek to suggest that he had been struck. All else was only imagination.

Day Two

Somewhat before sunrise there came again the sound of a soft clap as the chief instructor entered the bunkroom.

In an instant nearly all of us had sprung to our feet, scrambling for cover behind long curtains or under beds. The slower members of the group quickly recognized this as yet another test of their readiness as the drill instructor appeared and began pounding on the floor with the end of a large wooden staff. His thunderous hammering soon roused any late sleepers, and, when the lights came on a few seconds after the chief instructor's entrance, only two had still not left their hard-mattressed bunks. These two, of course, suffered the brunt of the drill master's harangue as, after washing, we all marched in silence to the meditation area.

Once again, we were instructed to sit facing the rising sun, quietly drawing strength from its rays. I remembered the events of the night before, and with renewed resolve and vigor, I rededicated myself to the cause that had prompted me to apply for this training. We then silently followed the leader through the morning stretch and loped off easily for the day's run.

The course on the first day had been south, and then to the east for the river crossing. This time we bore more to the right, following a bend in the road which led to the west, away from the swiftly running water.

The pace was somewhat slower than that of the day before, making it easier for even the weaker members of the party to keep up. Furthermore, there was more concern for the sore and blistered feet of the laggards than would have been expected from the behavior of the drill instructor on the previous excursion. He permitted the two new squad leaders to take care of "their men," and no longer lashed out physically or verbally at those who could not keep up.

After traveling less than a mile, we broke off the road and proceeded at a more rapid rate along a path which wound through the surrounding forest. At first it was fairly easy, the terrain being smooth and firm. Soon, however, the ground grew boggy, as if some southern tributary of the creek had wandered that way and lost itself in the gullies and washes, gradually making a morass of tangled undergrowth, vines, and fallen logs.

Here the path forked. The chief instructor led one group to the right, and the drill master led the other half off to the left on a spear of land drier than the rest. Following the all but invisible trails, the two teams made almost parallel progress through the swamp, playing a game of follow-the-leader deep into the forbidding muck and mire.

The trails soon converged in a walkway of two logs set side by side. Here and there, pilings had been erected to support this swamp-land dock, and in some places handrails had been constructed for balance.

As we penetrated deeper, the obstacles gradually grew more complex. First we came to a wall-climb barrier made of stacked pine logs. Forming two lines, we were encouraged to cross as quickly and safely as possible. First the two squad leaders from the previous day were sent ahead, to show the way and demonstrate how each obstacle was to be negotiated.

They hit the wall running as hard as they could, and their momentum carried them halfway up the wall. As gravity began to pull them down, each grabbed one of the heavy ropes that were attached to the topmost beam and began to walk up the wall or scramble up the rope as was needed to clear the top. Both did this by lying flat on the top and then sliding down the far side. Two by two we dashed forward, some easily following the squad leaders' example, others finding it necessary to clamber awkwardly, hand-over-hand, struggling every inch.

To drop into the soft earth on the other side required a fall of only a few yards, but there was a rope on that side for those who desired a slower descent.

As we sprinted up the shallow incline beyond the wall, it soon became apparent that this was the camp version of the "confidence course," so aptly named in military circles.

After climbing a ladder of log steps, we found ourselves on a low platform overlooking a particularly uninviting portion of the murky swamp. One of the squad leaders had already swung across it to a second platform some fifty feet away. Again, there were two ropes of sufficient width to permit a firm grip by even the least skilled of climbers, and these were equipped with large knots at each end for those who wished to stand or sit for the crossing. The trajectory of this apparatus was such that one could not help but make it across. The smoothness of the takeoff and landing, however, varied from student to student.

After the crossing we came to a huge fallen tree, its surface worn almost smooth by many feet, slanting upward at a forty-five degree angle into the branches of a great old black oak. Following one of the squad leaders and using the sturdy branches as convenient handholds and footholds, we climbed until we were lost in the leaves. The squad leader was the first to come upon the rope bridge. A single line attached by smaller cords to two rope handrails, it looked like a fragile thread which had been strung between two ancient trees high above the swamp (Figure 29).

The squad leader tested the line with his foot and visually inspected it before advancing. He told the group what to look for, advising us to check for wear or fraying and to remember that an enemy might weaken or booby-trap such a crossing point.

We crossed one at a time, with the chief instructor bringing up the rear. Huddled in a tight group, we faced the final set of obstacles.

At the command, we ran forward by twos, dodging and twisting through the posts planted vertically to test our flexibility and limberness. As soon as one representative of either group cleared, the next was dispatched.

We then ran up a small mound, made a leap to clear a water hazard, traversed the "monkey bars," a network of

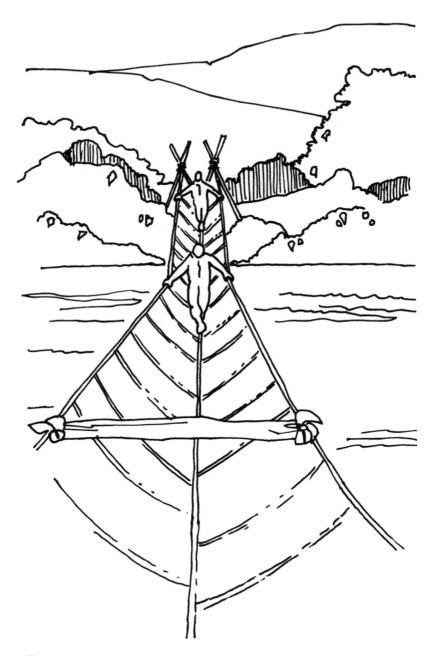

Figure 29. Rope bridge.

tree limbs permitting overhead crossing of a suspiciously overgrown puddle of lilies, and crossed a series of stumps jutting out of the mud to serve as stepping stones leading up and out of the mire and marshy land.

Through the grass and over or under a rail fence, through a low tunnel of vines and branches, a sprint to daylight, and we were done.

Everyone did well on the obstacle course except a few of the women members of the party, who had difficulty with those barriers requiring superior upper body strength, like the rope climb.

When we had caught our breath, the chief instructor signaled us to assemble, which we did quietly. He instructed us to move as silently as possible, as if on patrol or hunting, since there was a good deal of game in the area. Furthermore, he suggested we each select a walking staff from along the trail, which would make the journey easier, and which would also be required for the next phase of training. The stick was to be about shoulder height, about as thick as one's wrist, and straight, unless a fork was needed in order to use the stick as a crutch. Thorns and sharp points were not allowed.

As we walked slowly along, each of us chose from among a plenitude of branches, bamboo, and posts scattered about throughout the forest. Soon we were all hiking along, using our newfound "fingers" to probe and test the path.

Once we stopped to gorge ourselves on blackberries, which grew wild on brambles, and on grapes that hung from a mass of twisting muscadine vines nearby. Farther on, some late-blooming plums provided another feast. Around each of these area the guides pointed out the tracks of small game, deer, and fox, who had themselves probably been feasting shortly before our arrival.

THE BO (STAFF)

After a short march, we came to a small clearing and paused again to rest for a moment. The staffs were examined and evaluated by the instructors. The few staffs deemed unacceptable were modified or replaced.

"The bo, as it is known in Japanese martial arts," began the chief instructor, "is a wooden pole, six to eight feet long. Used as a weapon, the most effective part of the bo is the last six inches. Few are able to master proper use of the long pole, and we will not delve into all of the techniques used with this ancient device. We will, however, deal with the basic blocking and striking methods of the staff. These are handed down from ancient times and form the fundamental basis of bojitsu, or stick-fighting."

The chief instructor went on to detail the on-guard position, advance-guard position (much like that used with a rifle and bayonet), and the attention and at-ease stances. He demonstrated various methods of striking, such as the thrust; the jab, in which the rear hand shoots the front end of the bo out through the curled lead hand, spear fashion; and the slicing strike, made by using the forward hand as the pivot of a lever and jerking the rear hand upward, resulting in a much faster movement than the overhead strike. (See Figures 30, 31, 32, 33, and 34 for a two-man bo drill.) A few dirty tricks were revealed as well. For example, from the attention stance, holding the staff on one side, one could suddenly strike forward with the top without lifting the staff; or swing the lower end up with one hand between the enemy's legs. Targets were indicated and the practice form demonstrated.

"In olden times," the chief instructor explained, "Ninja trainees were not permitted to practice with weapons until they had achieved considerable skill at unarmed combat. In time of war, when it was necessary to raise an army quickly, agents were taught to make their own weapons as a part of their training.

"The bo staff is a natural weapon which comes easily to hand for the traveler. It is adequate defense against man or beast and has traditionally been the symbol of hidden knowledge and control, as in the shepherd's crook or the hermit's rod; and it may be carved with all manner of mystic symbols or totems. Furthermore, it may serve as a tent pole, fishing rod, or spear, and was certainly one of the first tools used by early man.

Figure 30. Two-man bo drill. Left: diagonal strike to the temple. Right: diagonal block.

Figure 31. Left: overhead block. Right: overhead strike.

Figure 32. Left: downward groin block. Right: uppercut strike.

Figure 33. Left: ready stance. Right: withdraw.

Figure 34. Left: side-stepping block. Right: straight thrust.

"The classic Shaolin bo was eight feet long. It was said that to be a master, one had to learn to use the last six inches only. Practice took many forms, from the traditional kata and drills to circling the edges of cups and saucers set against a wall or spinning small metal pinwheels set in sequence. The idea was to hold the far end firmly and rotate the tip with the leading wrist. Naturally, this developed powerful forearms, making the practitioner even more formidable in combat.

"We teach how to use the staff because it is a long-range weapon; because it is the symbol of wisdom; and because staff fighting is similar to both bayonet drill and rifle fighting, which are taught in advanced courses. It represents wood among the five elements, just as the ground is earth, the flame is fire, climbing in trees and on ropes is air, and tea is water. All are parts of the greater whole; all begin at this rudimentary level.

"Basically, the ends and tips are used for striking and the central portion serves as a shield and is used for blocking."

UNDERGROUND SANCTUARY

When everyone had completed the practice and had sufficiently grasped the principles and concepts of the two-man
stick-fighting form, the group was allowed to take a short
break. Relaxing quietly, we soon congregated near an old
well, similar to one outside the fence at the lodge, and began
to wonder aloud if there were potable water below, and if
so, how to go about retrieving it.

Most had learned the lesson of not drinking during or just
before class, since this can lead to nausea. And they never
gulped heavily after a hard workout, knowing this might
cause cramps as well as profuse sweating. The lesson of the
previous day, preparing the tea, participating in the ritual
sharing of the brew, had imparted to them the value of
enjoying each sip as if it were of tremendous importance,
which someday it might be. Still, they were tired enough to
appreciate a refreshing drink, and daring enough to ask permission to tackle the problem.

The instructors only smiled between themselves at this
turn of events, and produced from a concealed wooden
trunk nearby a length of stout rope and one of the peculiar
buckets made for drawing water from old-time wells,
weighted near the top so that it readily fell and filled.

A bucketful was withdrawn, and we all rinsed our hands,
cupped them, and drank a pure, cold draught together.

Several of the party were fascinated by the hidden tree
trunk, and were invited to investigate its construction. While
the drill instructor showed one group how to build the
hidden trunk, the chief instructor conspiratorially drew the
rest of us aside. He cautioned each one of us to silence, and
led us on hands and knees to the side of the well. Peeping
over the top, he raised himself up and slid slowly over the lip
of the restraining wall. My last sight of him was his masked
face, with one eye winking, descending into the well.

He was followed by the squad leader. When the rest of us
peered over the edge, we saw the chief instructor at the bottom of the pit, apparently standing on the surface of the
water near the wall! We climbed carefully down using pro-

truding handholds and niches unseen before due to lack of illumination.

When all of us had arrived, it could be seen that the chief instructor was standing on a narrow stone shelf, or lip, partially concealed by water, which ran around the interior circumference of the well. By standing on this shelf the instructor had created the illusion of walking on water. A step up from the shelf, about two feet above water level, a doorway had been made by removing stones from the wall (Figure 35). Following the chief instructor, we filed into a large underground chamber filled with crates, wooden boxes, cots, medical supplies, nonperishable foodstuffs—in short, everything one would need to survive a nuclear holocaust for an extended period of time. The air was fresh, circulated by some unseen pump, and the interior was cool and dry, perfect for long-term storage. The concrete block walls were about ten feet high, and the roof was reinforced steel.

Lighting a small candle, the instructor told us that, although there was a generator, it was not used during training sessions. As our eyes gradually adjusted to the gloom, however, the room was adequately illuminated by the one flame.

He explained that this secret sanctuary was based on an ancient plan of the Shaolin Hunan monastery, where the chief abbot was able to successfully defend the order by remaining hidden for some ten years. Construction was not so difficult as one might imagine. Since none of the materials could be brought down the well shaft, a large hole was dug near the well, the underground hideaway was built, and then it was simply covered back up. In this way, the workers were protected from cave-ins and the building went much more smoothly than if they had been tunneling underground. Asked why the water from the well did not intrude through the connecting tunnel, the chief instructor replied that the water table from which it drew its supply was far below the surface, and relatively stable. Also, because of the depth of the water table, the well water was exceptionally pure, having filtered through hundreds of feet of rock and sand.

Although no one admitted to being claustrophobic, the unnerving stillness of the bomblike storage room pressed

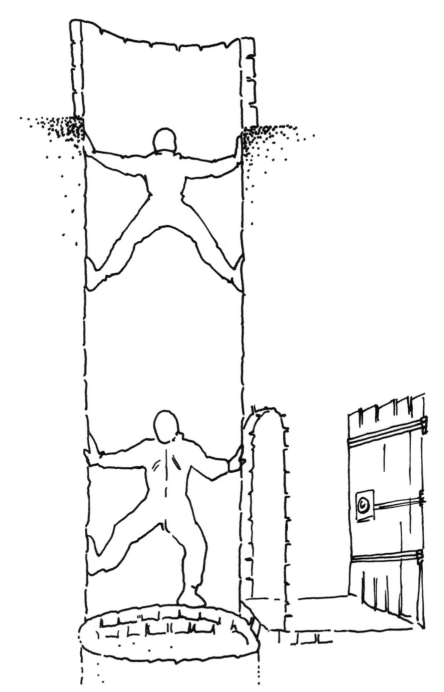

Figure 35. Underground bunker entrance.

upon us in spite of our having taken off our masks upon entering. The instructor went on to explain the intricacies of tunnel construction and the various ways in which chambers could be connected, concealed, and security trapped.

In Southeast Asia, the Viet Cong were known for their extensive use of tunnels. Some of these were traps rigged to collapse, some were used for storage, and some were employed to enter and leave urban areas from points far outside established city limits—and far from patrolling guards.

In Lebanon, it was reported that the Palestinian Liberation Front used prisoners as forced labor to construct an elaborate and intricate series of tunnels in, around, and under the streets of Beirut.

One of the students asked if the other wall, near the lodge itself, might not also be so equipped, possibly with a passageway to and from the House of Two Moons. The chief smiled and explained that it was considered bad form to perform the same trick twice, and then added cryptically, "But anything is possible."

There was a muffled noise beyond the cement-block wall, and the leader of the group waved everyone to cover before a quick flick of his hand extinguished the candle and plunged the chamber into utter darkness.

We remained still for several seconds, pressed against the walls, atop wooden boxes, behind crates, holding our breath, until a door in the wall opposite the well entrance opened and the drill instructor appeared carrying a hand torch and peered into the room.

In a flash, the chief instructor seized his wrist, pulled him into the room, and threw him on the floor with a resounding thud! The drill instructor scrambled to his feet and began laughing heartily. Soon they were both laughing and the teams were reunited.

Then we traded places, and the other team was led on a short tour of the area we had explored, while we were shown the adjoining chamber. This room was more elaborately furnished than the first. Weapons, low chairs, pillows, tables, a chess set, radio and television receivers, and short-wave equipment had obviously been there for a long time.

We learned that the other team had come in through a concealed entrance under a fallen black oak tree, beside the cache where the bucket and rope had been stored. It was their custom, the pair of instructors explained, to divide the classes and have them enter from both ends, to emphasize the complete concealment of the base of operations.

PUGIL STICK

"The purpose of pugil stick training is to develop confidence and aggressiveness in the individual soldier." The drill instructor's voice droned on, as it must have many times before, in front of hundreds of new recruits and trainees. We had left the underground stronghold and were assembled in a nearby pasture for training.

"This stick is a deadly weapon." He held aloft a wooden rod six feet long and an inch and one-half in diameter, padded with a cylinder of foam rubber on each end and in the middle, leaving a place for two hands to grip in the traditional manner. "In fact, even padded as it is, the training of agents in its use is no longer taught as part of the basic training for military service. This is because too many people got hurt with them. So be careful!"

The squad leaders began to hand out safety gear, taken from the hideaway, to their teams.

"We have taught you the basic striking and blocking techniques of the bo; all of these are applicable to the pugil stick. We shall equip you with sufficient body armor to protect you from serious injury, and give you an opportunity to see if you can apply what you have learned to an actual combat situation. All contestants are requested to do their best and protect themselves at all times."

A member of each team, appropriately suited and armed, was chosen by the drill instructor to begin. The two men entered the circle of students. At first they stood at the ready, but the drill instructor had them each place one end of the weapon to the ground and bow to the senior officer present, then to each other, before starting.

At first the combatants were somewhat hesitant, circling slowly or attempting half-hearted attacks in a probing manner, hoping to lure the opponent into some error of balance or judgment. The force of the blows increased with the level of intensity between the contestants.

Initially one might take a light blow on the shoulder or hip if the proper blocking sequence was not executed. Then, perhaps a moderate hit might land on the padded ski jacket which served as rib protector; or the head, wrapped in a full-coverage football helmet, complete with reinforced face shield, might be jarred by an extended attack. The hands and forearms, although protected just in case by heavy hockey player gloves, actually were struck very little.

There were, of course, no blows permitted below the waist, but this did not stop the unscrupulous from feinting an attack to the groin nor from trying to sweep an opponent's legs out from under him or simply tripping him. And not a few points were scored by pretending to stab at the foot or toes, then quickly whipping the far end of the pugil stick overhead onto the helmet or shoulder pads.

We battled for some time, sequential representatives of their respective teams taking the imaginary point count to and fro between them, with first one leading, then the other.

Finally, all the members of both sides had taken part except for John, a quiet young man who was standing on the sidelines. The drill instructor approached him with equipment required for the exercise, but John stepped back slightly and raised a palm to decline. On the other side, Jake, the anchor man of the team, seemed eager to continue his unbeaten winning streak.

The drill instructor insisted that the quiet one participate, but again he declined, citing nonviolence as his raison d'être. After still more insistence, his defense became that he had come only to learn, not to fight. This, of course, drew some criticism from his would-be opponent, who was obviously bent on provoking a confrontation, but John remained unperturbed. He declared that it made no difference to him who "won" such a contest, and that he could not see the necessity of risking injury to either party for the sake of scoring an arbitrary "point."

Still the drill instructor and Jake persisted, and some of John's teammates began to take their side. The pacifist denied their charge that it was cowardly to seek peace and to be satisfied with the two-man form practice; nor did he lack in the least the ability to defeat Jake, big as he was. The general lack of faith in John's statements, expressed as taunts and laughter, however, at last compelled him to accept the challenge.

"Hajime!" called the drill instructor, as he dropped his hand between the contestants, signalling them to begin.

Sensing an easy victory because of his opponent's unwillingness to fight, Jake charged forward strongly, feigning a ferocious attack to the head. John raised his forearms defensively, exposing his midsection—an error for which he paid the price when he received a swinging blow to the ribs. Although the jacket gave some protection, the impact of the blow caused him to bend forward at the waist.

Immediately, the aggressor seized the advantage and brought a vicious blow down on the back of John's head. Again, even though it was shielded by the helmet, the strike was forceful enough to drive John to the ground. Jake was preparing for the coup de grace, a downward stab with the bottom of the staff, when his hand was stayed by the chief instructor.

He and the drill master assisted the stunned contestant to his feet and assessed his state of consciousness by asking how many fingers they held up and whether he knew where he was. Apparently he answered correctly, since they declared a point for the other team.

As the winners cheered, John congratulated their unofficial corporal and returned to the ranks. One of his teammates asked him whether he was truly a martial artist, and, if so, what was his style?

"The way of not contending," he replied.

We wrapped up the session with a review, each of us striking or parrying with a staff against an imaginary enemy to the call of the drill instructor as the chief moved among the ranks correcting minor flaws or encouraging a student who was having a hard time. Practicing in this manner, we gradually came to realize that the sequence of movements was the practice form we had seen demonstrated earlier. By that time, of course, we had coordinated our movements into a smoothly flowing pattern, beginning and ending at the same point, which made continuous repetition both practical and possible. In this way, we spent the day until lunch.

Lunch consisted of wild cold salad, spiced by a few berries. Carrots, radishes, rice, and water were the staples, and I appreciated the wisdom of establishing such a cache when operating in the field. Generally speaking, we ate foods that could be found growing untended in the forest, although the stores were supplemented by a goodly supply in the underground bunker.

After stowing the pugil sticks and other equipment once more underground, we sat cross-legged on the pasture grass and listened to a slow relaxation litany designed to restore us to a meditative stance.

"All of you are merely pawns in the Great Game," the chief instructor was saying as we basked in the heat of the midday sun. "As such, you are expendable. The only way to survive is to become an asset to the powers that be. To accomplish this you must work together. The Chinese call this *gong he.*"

At his signal, we stood up and stretched slowly, regaining flexibility, and then gathered up our things to ready ourselves for the return trip. Turning north, the party made off in a ragged group. I was thankful that the instructors saw no need of returning through the swamp.

The pine forest gradually gave way to a forbidding forest, full of vines and gouged with ditches which had to be jumped or awkwardly negotiated. We kept to the rule of not-speaking and silent movement, enabling almost all to catch a glimpse of a large buck browsing lazily upwind of our position. His rack of antlers was impressive when he lifted his head to scan the surroundings as he munched, ears twitching this way and that alertly.

A little farther on, we met with an unfortunate accident. Dan, the squad leader, while foraging on the left flank, suddenly came upon a shallow ditch which happened to be the resting place of a pygmy rattlesnake. The viper wasted no time in striking out at the offender who had so rudely disturbed its rest, sinking its miniature fangs into his lower calf.

Dan cried out instantly, striking down so swiftly with his hand that he brushed the serpent off his leg in front of Lee and another woman, who were immediately behind him. They scampered for cover, but soon estimated the snake's size and potential danger and counterattacked, killing it with their staves. Lee then carried its body to the crowd which had gathered about the victim.

The chief instructor had Dan sit on the bank with his injured limb as low as possible and immobilized. Advising Dan to remain calm, he unzipped Dan's jumpsuit from ankle to knee and examined the wound. From inside his jacket, he produced a soft, green rubber package containing a field snakebite kit.

The fangs had penetrated the material of his coverall above his ankle-high, split-toed tabi boots. Their cloth uppers would have provided no protection at any rate. Pulling the field kit apart, the leader applied the suction cup part of the apparatus to the bite, two tiny punctures, little more than a half-inch apart and not overly deep, already somewhat red and angry looking. As the cup hung on the skin, drawing the venom outward, he slipped a loop of nylon line over the foot and above the wound. Pulling it snug by means of the slip-knot, he watched closely, tightening the cord only until it began to press into the skin.

Looking at his student, the instructor observed an expression of complete trust and almost perfect calm. He asked Dan how best to proceed, both of them knowing that medical help was more than an hour away, the safe time limit for using snakebite kit procedures alone. They discussed quickly that it was a slight wound, and not deep; but the life-threatening nature of the poison in Dan's system required immediate action to prevent it from reaching his heart.

They decided to cut.

While all of this was going on, the drill master had taken

several of the students aside and directed them to construct a stretcher, or litter, recognizing that the next item of business would be the rapid transport of the injured member back to the home base and on to a medical facility.

Two sticks were placed parallel to one another and three cross members half their length were lashed to them at a right angle (Figure 36). The central cross member was of greener wood than the rest, and so was soft and springy, yet strong enough to support the patient's lower back and hips. The two at either end were larger and more sturdy, designed to prevent the stretcher from folding inward with the patient's weight. John, who had apparently fully recovered from the pugil stick training incident, stripped off his coverall garment, revealing a pair of hiking shorts and V-neck T-shirt. This coverall served as the bed of the litter, and the wrists and ankles of the garment were used to tie the frame together.

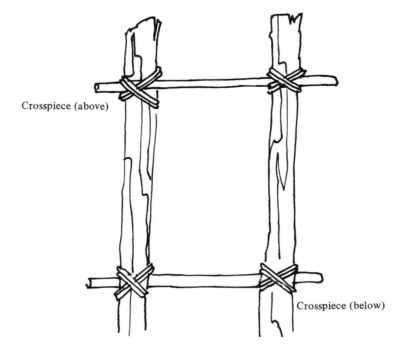

Crosspiece (above)

Crosspiece (below)

Figure 36. Stretcher construction.

"The tourniquet," began the chief instructor, as if giving a lecture in an ordinary classroom situation, "is not designed to restrict blood flow as is commonly believed. Rather its intent is to slow the circulation of lymph fluid, which lies in vessels just below the surface of the skin. If the tourniquet causes pain, redness, numbing, or paleness of a limb, it is too tight and must be loosened, but not released, until such symptoms subside."

He had withdrawn a razor-sharp triangular blade and a vial of antiseptic fluid from the other half of the kit. The small suction cup filled and fell away from the leg slowly enough to permit its removal and the emptying of its contents.

"Never make incisions on fingers or toes or over large veins," he mumbled to himself absently, crushing the plastic vial, wiping its liquid on the blade, then the wound, to disinfect the area. He made two incisions, one on each of the fang marks, one-quarter inch long and hardly an eighth of an inch deep. Wiping the area once again with the remaining antiseptic, he carefully squeezed out the suction cup and reapplied it over both cuts.

He then slipped the tourniquet down slightly, until it was about one and one-half inches above the injury. He asked Jane, a trainee who had medical experience, to stay with the patient, keeping him calm and watching the progress of the treatment. The lymph constrictor was to be removed for one minute every ten minutes during the return trip and reapplied slightly higher each time, or above any swelling that might occur. The pressure was to be released for half-hour intervals every two hours, and suction was to be applied until medical aid could be reached.

Dan had remained stoic throughout, partly because of his role in setting an example for the others, and partly because a man will cry out less in the presence of a woman. He reported no symptoms and did not appear overly pale or subject to going into shock. Nonetheless, professional medical help was essential.

The dead snake was to be brought along so that its specific venom type could be identified and the antidote properly supplied and administered. Jane noted the time on her watch and helped to seat the patient centrally on the litter. She and the chief instructor insisted he lie down, even though he appeared to be feeling quite well and not at all in distress. (Note: Before attempting first-aid treatment on a snake-bite victim, be sure you are well acquainted with the procedures as recommended by the Red Cross.)

It soon became apparent that the pasture in which we had been training was little more than an island in the middle of a considerable swamp. Both instructors were familiar with the terrain and quickly determined that the best route was due north. Although this would be a shorter evacuation trek, it would also necessarily take us over some difficult features of the landscape.

The instructors missed no opportunity to turn the misfortune into an effective lesson. Citing the medical emergency as a reason to move quickly, they elaborated a scenario in which the tactical mission was the rescue of an injured party. The chief instructor pointed out the additional considerations to be taken into account if the operation were to be carried out at night.

"First," he said, "travel through hostile territory at night can only be accomplished by means of a complete knowledge of the ground to be covered. When working with untrained individuals, marking the trail with glowing spots of florescent tape or a rope handline which can be easily followed is essential. Silence is hard to maintain for a limping individual or one in pain. Sometimes biting on a stick will help.

"Despite the difficulties, occasionally one must move at night, as when the enemy position has a clear field of fire, or when you are making an escape from captivity. At such times, move only far enough to get out of immediate danger. Remove the injured person to a safer area and tend to his wounds. Then go farther back out of enemy control until dawn and try to make it to friendly held territory during the day. Generally speaking, moving untrained or injured persons at night is not a good plan.

"An alternative method to the litter in use during this march is the one-man, or fireman's carry. For short dashes, the fireman's carry is a simple and effective method, assuming the victim does not have an abdominal injury. Stand with your right shoulder next to the victim's chest and centerline, at a right angle to his line of balance. Bend your right knee and set your right shoulder just below the victim's waist, reaching through his legs with the right arm to hold him around his right leg. Tip him over onto your back by pulling his right arm with your left arm, and lay his solar plexus on the back of your neck. His weight is now equally distributed on your shoulders and you can lift him easily by pushing with your right leg. This is good for short distances, but soon tires the carrier by suppressing his breathing with the weight and the slight chin lock.

"The sling carry is better for long distances, even if the victim is too weak to hold on or is unconscious.

"Have the victim hold onto his own wrists or bind them loosely together if he is unable to comply. Make a large loop out of a piece of stout line. If the victim is standing, wrap it around him so that the rope passes under his buttocks and the upper portion under his armpits. There are now two makeshift straps, one on either side of his body. If he is lying down, pass the line under him as indicated above to form the straps. Have the victim embrace your neck from behind, or place his tied arms over your head. If he is conscious, slip your arms through the straps, standing with his belly to your back, and lean forward slightly. Have him lift first one leg, then the opposite hand, and climb upon your back, riding on the upper portion of the pelvis. Have him cross his ankles to secure the "piggy-back" ride. This is made easier by the carrying straps, which help support the load.

"If the victim is unconscious, lie with one side to him and roll him over onto your back by means of the straps and his tied arms. Climb slowly to your feet from a hands-and-knees position and hold his thighs with both arms underneath, hands locked. Do not tie the ankles of an unconscious victim or one that is likely to pass out, as it may be necessary to drop him quickly to the ground, gently of course, in order to avoid enemy fire or detection. Also, his dead weight may throw you off balance, causing you to fall and become injured yourself. This makes it even more difficult to effect a successful rescue [Figure 37].

Figure 37. Sling carry method.

"If you and the victim must remain in hostile territory for an extended period of time, convey him to shelter, where he will be warm and dry, with fresh water.

"Fatigue of the carrier is always a factor when transporting wounded, especially with one-man carries. Whenever feasible, it is preferable to travel with walking wounded even though the progress be slow. Assuming that a man can carry twice his weight for half the distance he could normally walk before becoming exhausted, it follows that using more carriers to rotate that responsibility is simply good management of resources."

As we made our way through the forest, we talked about the responsibilities of one who administers first aid to the victim of an injury or accident. The teachers pointed out that most states had adopted "Good Samaritan" laws. The term comes from the Bible story of a traveler who, without thought of repayment or reward, and without regard for political or social considerations, had aided a wounded stranger on the road. Good Samaritan laws allow one to give aid to the best of one's ability in an emergency without being held legally liable for the consequences. In most cases, one should refrain from attempting any type of procedure with which one is not completely familiar. In most instances, making the victim comfortable and keeping him warm to prevent shock is all that should be done. Applying direct pressure to profusely bleeding or spurting wounds is all right if the patient is unconscious or unable to apply such pressure instinctively on his own. Holding the hands around a broken bone can often ease the pain and reassure the victim.

"Whatever course of action is pursued, one should never give up hope," counseled the chief instructor, "for whenever there is need, the strength will arise. To stop is to give up, to be swallowed in the dismal swamp of despair and self-pity. The world may be a jungle, but that does not mean one must live like an animal. Whenever two or more are joined in a cause, their power is more than doubled; and even when one is alone, he is with himself! Though you might have tried one thousand times, try once more. Lift the rock and you will find it, turn the corner and it is there. Never despair, there is always hope."

The litter bearers had equipped themselves with auxiliary harness straps to make their load easier to carry. Using the belts of several members of the group, they slipped loops over the long branches of the stretcher, then latched them together into a harness which ran under the arms and behind the necks of the forward and rear men (Figure 38). The chief instructor made sure the bearers were changed frequently. Many members of the class circulated around the procession, flanking guards staying out of the way of the main party but checking in often as we traveled through the forest. Everyone seemed to sense the urgency of the situation, and we moved fast even though our route was now uphill.

Figure 38. Carrying harness for stretcher.

At one point the incline was greater than 45 degrees, making normal carrying of the stretcher impossible. The drill instructor quickly replaced the rear man and, by lifting the end of the stretcher high against his chest, kept the patient on a level plane as we climbed. In front, two men each took hold of a side bar and carried it at ankle height, while a third unhitched the belts, fashioning them into a rope of sorts, which he used to lead the way up the slope, guiding and steadying the litter as it ascended.

The injured man had long since lain down. Turning his attention inward, he obviously willed himself to remain calm as he clung to the frame. His balance made it unnecessary to secure him to the litter. Once we had finally made it up the hill, we were on open ground, and we soon arrived at the camp area. We burst into the compound on the run.

Kneeling as we had been taught like a party of Indian braves, we waited near the periphery of the encampment as

Dan was carried on to the House of Two Moons. Most of us were breathing hard, but our respirations were not labored. The adrenaline of the life-and-death race through the wood coursed through our veins, and our thoughts went with our wounded comrade. In the distance we heard the sounds of confusion and clamor as the nature of the emergency was made clear to the household staff. When, soon after, we heard a Jeep or four-wheel-drive vehicle roaring off down the dirt road, we knew that everything possible had been done.

True to the *omerta,* or code of silence, we would not speak of the departed squad leader again until he returned, at which time we would act as if he had never left; no one would ask him where he had been or what he had done or seen. Only those who were authorized to receive his report would request information. Those with whom he wished to share a tale of the road would hear it when, and if, he was ready.

We watched, relaxed now, as the drill instructor slowly approached with Jake and John, the two men who had carried the stretcher from the periphery to the House of Two Moons. John was once again wearing his uniform. Several members of the class had gathered near the old stone well just outside the rail fence near the bunkhouse and were refreshing themselves with the cold, pure water from the deep spring that ran along the aquifer.

When we were all assembled and sitting comfortable on the hard-packed earth, the chief instructor spoke.

"Everyone has done well today. We," he indicated the drill instructor, "would like to thank each of you for performing in a professional manner during this crisis and hope that it was not overly uncomfortable for you." He paused and checked the level of the sun. "Since it is almost the hour of the evening meal, we will break early and regroup for dinner and the night class in the training hall." The drill instructor's nod confirmed this plan.

"Are there any questions before we disperse?"

There was a moment of silence, then a hand was raised.

"Sir," said a young man near the back of the group, "in

light of the mock attack last night, would we not be remiss in our observations if we did not consider the possibility that this, too, was a staged incident for our benefit?"

The drill instructor's lips drew back into a tight snarl and he started forward, but was restrained by the hand of the senior leader.

"No," he said softly, smiling.

"But how can we be sure of that?" continued the questioner.

"The proof is in the snake," was his answer.

"Sir?"

"The snake," said the chief instructor, "is dead. Being a follower of the Way, it would be against my principles to let you kill one of my snakes unless it were necessary. Certainly not for a class, or money. For all life is precious, nor can any be replaced."

Surveying the crowd, he gathered that this explanation was not sufficient, and so carried on.

"The test of reality in this world is touch. Your eyes can deceive you, your ears confuse. In the legend of Chuang Tzu the question is posed, are you a man dreaming of being a butterfly, or a butterfly dreaming you are a man? Only by reaching out into the darkness and touching can we know if a thing is material or noncorporeal. Did you not touch the snake? Feel the dry scaliness of its skin? The sticky wetness of its blood?"

"No sir."

The chief instructor laughed out loud. "Why not? Are you not here to learn to gather intelligence? To see and remember? And carry the information to others?"

The young man hesitated before replying, "I was afraid."

"A man may believe whatever he wishes, despite incontrovertible evidence to the contrary. The only thing better than a well-told lie is a true story no one believes." The chief instructor smiled wickedly.

ESCAPE AND EVASION

After dinner we gathered in the old barn. Having performed the entering ritual, we sat watching the sensei demonstrate the techniques of that evening's class.

"We have said that we teach you here not so much a martial art as a way of surviving. We do not train expendable agents for suicide or one-way missions. In every instance, the mission is unfinished until the agent has returned and is successfully debriefed."

He adjusted his glasses.

"However, infiltration of hostile territory, be it city or country, and penetration of the enemy stronghold by means of covert entry for the purpose of surreptitious operations is not without its hazards. We have spoken of seppuku as a means of dealing with torture and imprisonment. Let us now speak of ways to avoid capture. We have said that the various methods of rolling are means whereby one may vanish quickly and escape, even at very close range. But suppose the enemy guard does get the drop on you. He may order you to halt, or freeze. Even in a foreign language, such a command is understandable.

"The sentry may demand identification or the proper password. Sometimes, when masquerading in the uniform of an enemy officer, it is possible to bluff a security guard long enough to get near him and attack. If the current, or even a dated, password is known, one may use it to confuse the enemy about one's identity."

Sand-in-Eyes Technique

"When confronted by an armed sentry, remain as calm and relaxed as possible. If you look fearful, he will feel strong and may be lured into overconfidence. If you look strong, he will be fearful and more careful. In order to secure more complete control, the guard will demand that you put up your hands.

"On the command *hands up!* if he is within range—from two to ten feet from you—immediately swing both arms up with hands extended, palms facing down, as if to follow the order as quickly as possible.

"As the right hand rises, let the closed right fist open and the fingertips extend toward the enemy's face, releasing a

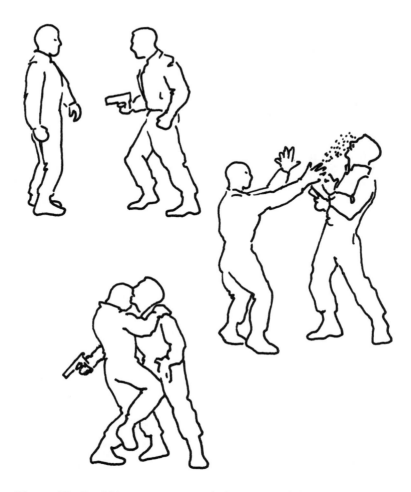

Figure 39. Sand-in-eyes escape technique. Aim for the point of the chin.

handful of sand or dirt into his eyes to temporarily blind him. If you did not have time to pick up any sand before he caught you, let him get close enough to touch his face with your extended hand, making him tilt back and blink. And if he is very close, swing the back of your fist up under his chin to stun him for an instant.

"Run, or grab the weapon with one hand and close with him, striking a vital point to take him down [Figure 39]."

98

Side-Kick Technique

"Suppose the enemy has succeeded in covering you with his weapon and has approached to consolidate his position [Figure 40]. From the hands-up pose, watch him closely as he comes into range. If he carries his rifle low, or at hip level, there may be an opportunity to disarm him by grappling for the weapon. If the sentry places the gun at your chest, or prods the stomach with his barrel, he is vulnerable.

"Pivot on the heel of the left foot, twisting the body sideways to move the torso out of the line of fire. Drop both hands swiftly downward and seize the barrel in a viselike grip. Jerk the rifle forward, causing him to resist by pulling back. Suddenly reverse your pull and jam the butt of the weapon into his stomach. In most cases pulling on the gun will not cause him to fire. He is more likely to try to maintain control by not doing so.

"Pull forward again and execute a powerful side kick to his midsection, snatching the rifle out of his hands as he is pulled into the force of the blow [Figure 41]. If he hangs on, swing your kick around clockwise to throw him down [Figure 42].

"Strike downward with the butt of the rifle to the base of the skull to finish him off."

Figure 40. Side-kick technique.

Figure 41.

Figure 42.

Wheel-Throw Technique

"Should you be taken prisoner under circumstances that prevent a quick escape, sooner or later the sentry will find it necessary to transport you to a holding area or place of confinement.

"You are in the hands-up position [Figure 43] when the sentry issues the command to move out, swinging the butt end of his rifle to indicate the direction of march. This brings him to the military position of port arms, with the weapon diagonally across his chest.

"Drop both hands and grab the weapon while it is not pointing at you. Jerk it to yourself as if trying to get it away from the enemy, causing him to resist by pulling back [Figure 44]. Slam the upper end of the weapon into his face or side of the head to disorient him.

"Sit down quickly, pulling him forward over you by his hold on the rifle, and kick upward into the groin or stomach with either or both feet [Figure 45]. Block his ankles and continue to pull him over, supporting him with the legs, and kick him to one side or over your head.

"If he clings to the rifle, he will land heavily on his back [Figure 46]. This will knock the wind out of him, making it possible for you to escape or finish him off.

"The counter to this trick is a forward roll."

Figure 43. Wheel-throw technique.

Figure 44.

Figure 45.

Figure 46.

Hangman-Hold Technique

"If the sentry is alert and intelligent, he will carry his weapon at shoulder level. This indicates that the best target for him is the head. He may be enticed into coming into range, or he may come within range of his own volition in an effort to intimidate you [Figure 47].

"Since the head is a small target, a quick movement can sometimes effectively save the day. Side-step to the left and execute a mirror block, catching the barrel, and deflecting it simultaneously [Figure 48]. Swing the captured gun down in a circular motion in an effort to wrest it from his grasp. When the weapon is vertical, snap the lower end into the enemy's groin to disable him and break his balance.

"Pivot on the ball of the left foot, continuing to circle the weapon down and around in a clockwise manner as you step through between yourself and your pivot point [Figure 49]. This action will spin the enemy around with you as you turn so that you and he end up back to back. Reaching back over your head, hook the rifle under the enemy's chin in front of his throat and jerk it toward the back of your neck. Bend forward, lifting him off the ground and choking him with his own weight [Figure 50]. He may be thrown by strongly pulling him all the way over and will land flat on his chest and face.

"The counter movement is an aerial back roll, landing on the feet."

Figure 47. Hangman-hold technique.

Figure 48.

Figure 49.

Figure 50.

Distraction

"One of the oldest tricks in the book for distracting the enemy's attention is to make him think you are not alone. Observe whether he is watching carefully and has good eye contact. If so, he is vulnerable. When he comes within range, look over his left shoulder. One must practice this to make it believable; pick an object or spot to look at. Imagine the approach of a friend. If unmasked, use facial expression to sell it [Figure 51].

"He may turn his head to look for himself, or he may say, 'That's the oldest trick in the book.' If he is disbelieving, look again and nod as if signalling to an unseen ally. Sometimes a slight noise will occur to give your ruse credibility.

"Pivot on the heel of the left foot and the ball of the right, twisting the body to one side, out of the line of fire, as you chop down onto his wrist with the edge of your near hand [Figure 52]. A sharp blow will frequently make him drop the weapon.

"Step into him, dropping both arms over his extended arm to secure a good hold, and follow up in case he is not disarmed by the chop [Figure 53]. Try to knock him over with your shoulder and hip.

"Continue turning and pulling him around and over your lead leg, forcing him to fall on his back. If he is still armed, execute a wrist lock to force him to release the gun." [Figures 54, 55]

Figure 51. Distraction technique.

Figure 52.

Figure 53.

Figure 54.

Figure 55.

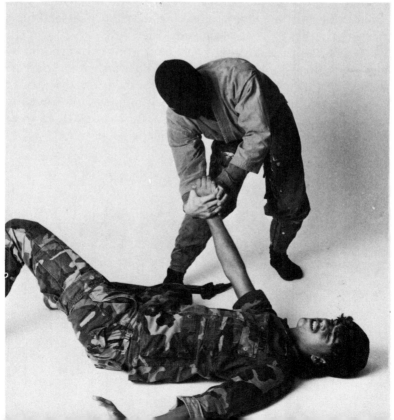

Low-Block Turning Escape

"This technique is effective when an armed sentry does not approach from the front, or orders his prisoner to turn around before approaching. It works equally well against rifle or pistol.

"It is a little known fact that a man can turn faster than he can pull a trigger. This is due to the inherent time-lag factor of the human brain between seeing, deciding, and acting. A second factor that makes this move effective is the fact that by turning one twists the body out of the line of fire, so that even if the weapon is discharged, the projectile will miss the intended target.

"When the touch is made and the position of the weapon becomes known, suddenly spin around while executing an elbow block, slapping down on the enemy's arm or weapon and deflecting it aside. Step forward with the left foot and grab the wrist of the sentry [Figures 56, 57]. Drive your other hand into his elbow, breaking the elbow or securing a straight-arm bar to control the gun [Figure 58].

"Break his arm over your knee, or continue to turn him by means of the arm bar, tripping him forward over your extended left leg to land heavily, face down, on the ground [Figure 59]. Here he may be disarmed, pinned, and forced to submit by means of the wrist lock. The customary coup de grace is a vertical chop to the back of the neck."

Figure 56. Low-block turning escape.

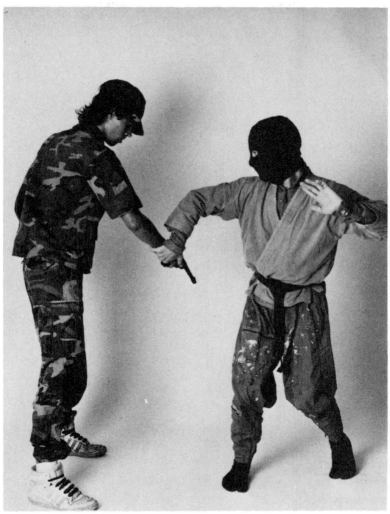

Figure 57.

Figure 58.

Figure 59.

High-Block Turning Escape

"The sentry who places his gun at the back of the head or neck to control his prisoner makes himself vulnerable to a swift turning attack. Remember that you can turn faster than he can pull the trigger, and that turning will also pull your head out of the line of fire. Suddenly jerk around with your near arm, executing a mirror block and striking and deflecting the enemy pistol or forearm [Figures 60, 61].

"Let your arm continue to circle down and inward, hooking over the enemy's arm and, if necessary, pin it to your body by wrapping your arm about his elbow. Grab his sleeve or biceps to keep the weapon away and the danger minimal.

"Pull the sentry forward by means of the entangling arm lock and drive a powerful side kick into his midsection to drive the air out of his lungs and render him helpless. The impact of this strike is doubled due to the simultaneous force of the pull forward and the strike outward [Figure 62].

"If the opponent is too close after the deflection for the side kick, shift further into him by turning still more and strike with the heel of the palm to the chin and the knee to the groin."

Figure 60. High-block turning escape.

Figure 61.

Figure 62.

Escape from Gun to Head

"The enemy may wish to intimidate you by pointing a knife or gun at your face [Figure 63], throat, or solar plexus. If this happens, try to incite the opponent to extend his arm as far as possible. Psychologically, this is a demonstration of the extent of his power or control. If he can be made to lean forward, that too is beneficial. Whether your hands are up or down, suddenly pivot sideways out of the line of fire and deflect the weapon to the side with a cross-chest block [Figure 64]. Against a knife, obviously, strike the wrist or forearm. Let yourself fall forward to close with the sentry before he can pull away and recover his balance. If he is close enough, strike with the knee; if he is at extended range and has a rifle, lash out with a snap kick.

"In most cases, these actions will bring you close enough to entangle the enemy's arm or arms with your other hand, helping to maintain control of the weapon. Strike out with a reverse chop to the throat of the guard, stunning him and possibly causing his death [Figure 65].

"Follow with a takedown to lower him to the ground, and carry the body to a place of concealment."

Figure 63. Escape from gun pointed at head.

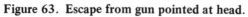

Figure 64.

Figure 65.

Unmasking Escape

"Inevitably, the hooded agent must face the possibility of being captured, restrained, and unmasked," the sensei told us. "Some masks are designed to cover the lower half of the face and will be pulled down to reveal the face beneath. The customary hood must be pulled off the top of the head. Those which cover only the eyes are jerked to one side. Some schools advocate wearing a hideous demon mask beneath the cloth to temporarily startle the opponent, providing a moment to escape. Other styles teach their students to hide a dart or 'spitting needle' in the mouth to shoot at the guard. And there are those in the professional wrestling ranks who can spray a green mist from their mouths when hopelessly trapped.

"For the purpose of making the enemy blink, however, it is sufficient to spit in his face, or in the eye if one is practiced. During this second of confusion, one may often escape. In practice, it is equally effective to simulate this unhygienic attack by merely blowing or puffing on the partner [Figure 66]. If this is done unexpectedly, it can even make one familiar with the technique flinch.

"If the hands are tied, in front of or behind the body, strike out strongly with a snap kick to the groin, disabling the sentry [Figure 67]. Finish him with a knee kick to the head." [Figure 68]

Figure 66. Unmasking escape.

Figure 67.

Figure 68.

Ninja Bullet Evading Tricks

"Since the introduction of the firearm to warfare, most other weapons have fallen by the wayside. Considering that pistols are probably the most frequently encountered item of this genre, we should reflect for a moment on methods for overcoming them.

"In ancient times, the problem of how to dodge the crude lead balls of the flintlock era was addressed as a simple extension of dodging arrows or spears. This was especially true of the handgun, since a man could fire only one shot before the agent could bridge the gap between the shooter and the target and overcome him. In the modern era, the automatic, semi-automatic, and basic revolver all present a more complicated issue.

"First, consider the man behind the weapon. Is he trained or unskilled? One may determine this by his stance. An amateur holds his gun near his body, while the professional points it at arm's length. Eye contact is another clue. A good gunman will keep his eyes on his target, letting his peripheral vision take in movement around him. His manner will also indicate the extent of his training. Police officers and others accustomed to giving orders shout simple commands, or use low, menacing tones to get their message across. High-pitched yells and signs of hesitancy indicate lack of authority.

"The techniques we have shown here *may* work against even a competent gunman. However, they are not recommended for use against a trained shooter. Some of these methods depend almost entirely on the common tendency of the amateur shooter to miss instinctively. Professionals have put in enough practice on the firing range to suppress or eliminate such errors.

"In dealing with rifles," the sensei continued, "it must be remembered that they are most effective at a range which makes approach if not altogether impossible, then at least difficult. In an enclosed area, however, a rifle may be jumped just like any other firearm, and its larger size may be turned to disadvantage.

"When held at gunpoint with the weapon aimed at your chest at a range too great to be bridged quickly, watch the hammer or the trigger finger of the shooter. As he fires his round, pivot on the heel of either foot and turn the body sideways to present a smaller target, and fall back out of the line of fire. In the arrow-catching trick, the catcher strikes out with his lead hand to snatch the shaft from the air in conjunction with this movement. Essentially, it turns the body out of the line of fire.

"When held at gunpoint with the weapon pointed at your head, drop flat to the belly by kicking back with both feet simultaneously as discharge of the firearm is imminent. The first shot will miss, being too high. Immediately execute a side roll out of the line of fire. If the enemy fires down on you, the second shot should also miss, as there is a tendency to overshoot when shooting downward.

"Another trick which takes advantage of this tendency entails rolling forward toward the enemy as he fires down, in an effort to close with him.

"Conversely, there is a normal instinct to undershoot, or shoot below, a target above the head, as many a duck hunter will testify. Take into account the time-lag factor between seeing, deciding, and acting, as well as the problem of raising the weapon to a difficult angle, and you will understand that the shooter aiming at an overhead target is at a disadvantage. Distract the sentry by throwing something over his head, or by looking over his shoulder at an imaginary partner; his weapon will drop slightly whenever he turns. Cartwheel or handspring forward to cover the ground between you, and execute a flying side kick, or tobi-geri, to his head or throat before he can react. Such gymnastic tricks cover the distance quickly and present an unusual and distorted target to the enemy."

We practiced all the rifle techniques by substituting our walking staffs for the firearm. Pistols were simulated by pointing fingers, and restraints by having the "prisoner" interlock his or her fingers.

The sensei stressed that the methods employed were not designed to be taught as a martial art, since most of the students had already had at least a modicum of that type of training elsewhere and probably were pretty well aware of how to fight, kill, or subdue an opponent. All of these techniques were designed to permit the user to retake control of a situation in which he appeared to be a helpless victim, and thereby either escape or turn the tables on the capturing party. For law-enforcement officers, this was particularly important so that they might be on guard against the tricks taught by the sensei. For the agent in hostile territory, a sudden break for freedom before it became necessary to escape from confinement or prison might mean the success or failure of the mission.

Each technique is intended to take advantage of the tiniest opportunity, whether it is created, like the sand-in-face ploy, or accidental, in order to disarm, disable, or escape from the enemy before he can get off a shot which might cause injury or raise an alarm.

"These are not all of the possible combinations," the sensei concluded, "nor do they represent any specific style or system. They have been gleaned from centuries of criminal and clandestine operations, and taught to members of the Japanese underworld and the Ninja for self-defense and self-protection."

When the practice was over, the sensei had us resume our seats on the tatami mats for the closing meditation. Closing our eyes, we sat quietly for a time, listening to our breathing.

"The subject of this evening's meditation is the Samurai Creed," intoned the hypnotic voice of the sensei. It seemed he spoke to each person individually, whispering in the ear of every student his quiet directions and the text of the lesson.

"Mentally repeat after me each phrase, so that the code will be subconsciously imprinted upon your memory."

I have no parents; I make the Heavens and the Earth my parents.
I have no home; I make the tan tien [hara] *my home.*
I have no means; I make docility my means.
I have no magic power; I make personality my magic power.

I have neither life nor death; I make A Um [inhalation and
  exhalation] *my life and death.*
I have no body; I make stoicism my body.
I have no eyes; I make the flash of lightning my eyes.
I have no ears; I make sensibility my ears.
I have no limbs; I make promptitude my limbs.
I have no laws; I make self-protection my laws.
*I have no strategy; I make the right to kill and to restore
  life my strategy.*
I have no designs; I make seizing opportunity my design.
I have no miracles; I make righteous laws my miracles.
I have no principles; I make adaptability my principles.
I have no tactics; I make emptiness and fullness my tactics.
I have no talent; I make ready wit my talent.
I have no friend; I make my mind my friend.
I have no enemy; I make incautiousness my enemy.
I have no armor; I make benevolence my armor.
I have no castle; I make immovable mind my castle.
I have no sword; I make no mind my sword.

Here he paused dramatically, allowing the litany to deeply
settle into the brains of his audience, then continued.

I am nothing . . .
O sensei, help me to learn the Way.
Teach me to be one who knows.
May I live to serve your higher purpose,
In this strand of time.

His voice trailed off and each was left to his or her private
reverie for at least as long as the chant had taken to recite.
I heard no one cough, speak, or shift position in any way during this session. Our weariness and the previous night's training made it easy to be comfortable for as long as the period
lasted.

Finally, the soft voice in the shadowy darkness suggested
that everyone inhale slowly and deeply, and gradually we returned to consciousness and material reality.

I slept well that night.

Day Three

With the dawn came meditation, followed by the morning run. On this occasion we traveled due south, so that during our stay we explored virtually the entire field below the lodge site, first east across the creek, then west through the swamp, and now past that cut-off and deep into the dense forest farther still down the trail.

By this time most had acclimated themselves to the regimen as well as the pace, and so the journey did not seem as far as it had the first day, although it must have been a good two miles. Finally, we broke off the trail and headed cross country, necessarily causing the group to become more dispersed and the pace to slow somewhat. We ran easily, staves held loosely in hand, eyes scanning ahead. Almost all of us displayed the stoic mannerisms of hunters and woodsmen as we rushed through the undergrowth in simulated tribal band fashion.

Soon the terrain funneled us once more into loose single file, strung out—since the instructors had been specific in their teachings not to bunch up—roughly ten yards apart. We had been climbing steadily upward on a slight grade when the trail suddenly gave out and we found ourselves on a precipice facing a drop of some twenty feet.

Forced to jump to avoid being overrun and pushed off the precipice by the next student in line, I had just enough time before my leap to catch a glimpse of the chief instructor below, directing the trainee who had just landed to circle back and make the jump again.

The way we landed in the soft earth pit and instinctively rolled to dissipate the impact confirmed to the teachers that the dojo training had been well spent. Despite having to perform this test of judgment and physical prowess no less than three times, not a single student sprained an ankle, twisted a knee, or jammed a hip. This part of our training was based in part on parachute landing methods used in Airborne or Ranger classes. Those who had actually participated in this training could be identified by their practiced tuck-and-roll landing, designed to prevent the chutist from becoming entangled in the shroud lines.

We ran on again, uphill, until we broke into a wide clearing beside a large, clear lake. Being at the northern end, we observed a wooden bridge and culvert through which the overflow of the retained water spilled quietly, disappearing into the forest to form the swamp through which we had trekked the previous day. Continuing to observe the rule of silence, we melted into the surrounding trees and bushes at the chief instructor's signal to fan out.

Rodney, the remaining squad leader (the drill instructor had assumed command of Dan's team after he was disabled), was dispatched by the chief instructor to check out the area.

We watched as the man slithered forward, noting every action he took to conceal himself and observe the lakefront without being seen. It soon became apparent that he was practicing his concealment technique on the wildlife that had come there to drink and socialize. He made an effort to remain in sight of the class whenever possible, knowing we would be following his example, and pointed out several natural hazards, such as the huge wasp nest suspended beneath the bridge by its anchoring stem. Despite his proximity, he was not attacked or stung. Perhaps the mental imagery of the hexagram was in operation at that moment.

Completing this reconnaissance, he slipped across the bridge and waved an arm to signal the group. Invisible trainees quickly materialized out of the wood with the two instructors and crossed lightly over the wooden bridge without setting off the insect alarm.

Having arrived at the site, everyone sat or knelt at ease awaiting the morning's lesson. By now, we had come to appreciate the chance to rest whenever possible, since one seldom knew how long it would be until the opportunity presented itself again.

FIELD OPERATIONS

The chief instructor now began to speak. "Assuming that the agent is parachuted in—since this is the best way to penetrate the enemy perimeter without detection—it is essential that he be equipped with a minimum of superfluous devices and gear. For maximum efficiency, he should be able to use his harness and parachute cloth for secondary purposes after landing. Parachuting into enemy territory is a modern extension of the Ninja's traditional predilection for striking at the enemy from unexpected angles and across impassable barriers, natural or otherwise. With our plunge over the cliff, we have simulated a parachute landing. Now, for the purposes of our training excercise, we have successfully 'penetrated enemy territory.'

"Once the enemy territory has been penetrated," the chief instructor told us, "the agent will customarily establish a base camp in a remote or hidden location. There, he will conceal all evidence of his presence and mission, and assume the cover identity from which he will operate.

"To secure his headquarters against search or discovery, the agent will establish a security perimeter and a route whereby he can enter the encampment safely. Booby traps and alarms may be used for the security perimeter.

"The principle of avoiding traps and snares by taking a hidden or circuitous route is apparent in the ritual of entering any Ninja encampment. A specific series of steps and stops is required, not only to make obeisance to a particular deity or ancestor, but also as a way of remembering the safe path from point to point. As previously indicated, this procedure also serves as a silent recognition signal.

"A very simple, yet effective, device, with the added advantage that it does not reveal the presence of a camp, is the ankle pit, a hole or depression twelve to eighteen inches deep, with a few twigs over the top and covered with leaves or pine needles. It must be constructed in such a way that, should the enemy fall into it, he will sprain or disable either the knee or ankle, and camouflaged so that when this unfortunate event occurs, there is no evidence of a trap. Such traps discourage pursuers by forcing them to move very slowly.

"A logical next step is the 'tiger pit,' made by planting pointed stakes upright in the bottom of the pit. The stakes are designed to pierce the foot of the hapless intruder who blunders into the trap. A tiger pit would not be found too near a base camp, since its obvious construction and intent would give away the fact that someone was in the area. Furthermore, the time it takes to build a tiger pit might be better used on the mission."

BASE CAMPS

"Shelter has more than one meaning for the Ninja," continued the head instructor. "In addition to serving as protection from wind, rain, snow, heat, cold, and insects, it also acts as a jumping-off point for the covert operation and as a cache for secret weapons or 'last-stand' devices. Remember, part of the mission may be to disrupt the enemy supply, communication, or transport lines. In such an instance, an extended stay may be necessary. Many times the agent of old would run all night, hole up during the next day, resting, waiting, and recouping his strength, and then emerge at night like some ancient vampire. His eyes would be adjusted to the darkness since he had not come out all day. Likewise, his senses would be heightened by sensory deprivation as well as by the esoteric or mystical practices he employed. In short, he would be at the peak of his power, focussed solely on his objective, while his enemy would be preparing to retire for the evening and would be prey to the myriad demons of superstition that haunt the night.

"In addition to cover and concealment, shelter must provide protection from extremes of weather. The Ninja, seeking to disturb as little as possible, makes efficient use of caves, hollow trees, overhangs of rock, and trees. Even a thin layer of sand or leaves may be adequate.

"The modern survivalist is apt to carry a solar blanket, a thin sheet of reflective Mylar, which serves as shelter and bedding and can be folded into a handkerchief-size packet. Commandos and parachutists make use of the parachute to construct simple tents or a version of the Indian tepee. To make a tepee, several poles over ten feet long are tied together with a thong or rope which is fitted through a hole at one end of each pole. Then the poles are spread out, fanlike, to form a frame. For proper construction, two or more poles are set outside the tent in tripod or bipod support fashion. One of the parachute seams is slit to form a door flap, and the grommet holes from which the shroud lines descend are pegged to the ground with short sticks. Such a structure can withstand winds of ten to twenty miles an hour, rain, and insects. A small fire in the center of the circular interior will be shielded from wind and weather, and its smoke will rise upward and out the improvised chimney. The parachute is well suited for survival treks, since it can be rolled up and carried along over the shoulder.

"The Ninja chutist usually buries his parachute along with his 'traveling clothes,' or jumpsuit. If he retains them for the mission, the chute is used more like a blanket than a shelter, for reasons of camouflage.

"An effective shelter may be quickly constructed by tying down a small sapling or tree to form a tunnellike alcove. Build the fire at the entrance to conserve heat and act as a barrier to insects. The leaves or pine nettles will act as rudimentary shingles, allowing rain or snow to collect and run off without penetrating. In the morning, the boughs may be released and the surroundings returned to their natural state.

"Ninja are known for the construction of elaborate underground burrows and tunnels. The danger of cave-ins is ever-present in the digging and maintenance of such shelters. Underground shelters need not be elaborate, however; a shallow depression, no more than six inches deep, may serve as a temporary abode, covered with a blanket, if one is available, or, if not, by a thin layer of soil, leaves, or nettles to conserve heat [Figure 69]. Be careful of ground-burrowing insects and spiders.

"Observe the direction of prevailing winds by the way in which trees have grown. When undersides of leaves are seen, a storm is in the offing. Build your shelter in such a way that it naturally deflects the wind around you. Believers in the mystic applications of covert operations orient themselves

Figure 69. Ankle-deep pit (best under leaves).

north to south for magnetic continuity. If yours is to be a long-term operation, stay near food and water supplies.

"The knee-deep pit is shelter in a pinch, but it is the principle of kneeling or squatting and hugging the knees to the chest to conserve body heat which is really the crux of this technique. In snow, one may survive for short periods by burrowing under the powder to make a 'rabbit hole,' just large enough for the body. By packing the snow into solid walls, the nook can hold enough heat to prevent frostbite and exposure injuries [Figure 70].

"A popular trick of ancient Ninja was to emulate the trap-door spider by lying in wait for his prey in a pit roofed with a shallow tray of earth. With the roof in place, the earth appears to be unbroken, concealing the hip-deep pit in which crouches the agent [Figure 71]. When the enemy comes within reach, the Ninja flings up the roof, seizes the sentry, and pulls him into the hole to be killed. In this way, the sentry vanishes from his group and can be impersonated by the agent, disguised in his uniform. If the agent suddenly leaps out of the pit and strikes, it is considered an 'appearing' technique rather than a shelter or trap."

NESTING IN TREES

"Hiding or sleeping in trees has several advantages over sheltering in any sort of ground cover. Because people seldom look up, and because the leaves of the tree will partially mask the sky beyond, the problems of camouflage are minimized.

Figure 70. Knee-deep pit (useful under snow).

Figure 71. Hip-deep pit.

"In some climates, arboreal perches are selected because they are above the normal flying range of mosquitoes. Some trees make better habitats than others, but all must be inspected for insects, such as ants, wasps, and bees. Palm fronds can be knitted together to make a semipermanent structure; palm fronds, however, are favored by roaches, and are very fragile. Japanese snipers used palm-tree shelters extensively during World War II.

"There are various ways to rest in a tree. Using the tiger or lion style, one lies along a limb, loosely hooking the ankles and wrists for support [Figure 72]. The bear method, used on pine trees, is to straddle the bole and hook a leg over two opposing limbs. A popular method with hunters, especially in oaks, is to sit on a large limb with legs folded, leaning with the back against the tree trunk [Figure 73].

"Do not be concerned about falling out of the tree when sleeping in any of these poses. At first, the fear alone will keep you awake. After a while, you will fall into a light sleep while still maintaining enough alertness to prevent accidents. With practice, one can sleep soundly without shifting enough to topple over."

Figure 72.

Figure 73.

AMBUSH TECHNIQUES

"Having established his hideout and secured it by camouflage and booby-trap alarms, the agent would begin his mission.

"Making his way toward the objective, he would reconnoiter the terrain, noting any features which might impede the advance of friendly troops, as well as cataloging any and all hostile forces and their positions. Such intelligence information would be invaluable to a commander in the field.

"Ordinarily, a solo agent—meaning one operating independently but not necessarily alone—would avoid contact with enemy forces by means of the inpo techniques we have already discussed and practiced rather than risk exposure. However, there are times, such as when one wishes to incite terror or anxiety in the enemy troops, when one might want to ambush a patrolling guard for the purpose of interrogation. The captured soldier could then be set free or 'allowed to escape' to race back to his superiors with the knowledge that a Ninja was in the area, thereby leading the agent to his headquarters. Or the captive could simply vanish, creating doubt whether he is absent, injured, or dead.

"To ambush the enemy is to attack him unexpectedly from a concealed position in such a way that he is neutralized quickly and quietly. Striking from ambush increases the probability of success by 30 percent. Damage done by a surprise attack is 20 percent greater, due to the decreased reaction time of the victim.

"To attack the patrolling sentry from above, select an overhanging projection, such as the eave of a roof, a rock cliff, or a large tree limb which extends over the trail or frequently used path. The sentry, unaware of the impending attack, passes beneath the agent while on patrol or because it is his custom to use this path.

"It is a little-known fact that most people seldom look above shoulder height when walking, and rarely look up unless their attention is attracted in that direction. The agile Ninja takes advantage of this principle when attacking from above.

"Lying along the limb in the lion posture, the camouflaged Ninja is completely concealed by the surrounding leaves and the nonreflective coloration of his uniform [Figure 74]. With slow, regular breathing exercises, he gradually becomes one with the tree, and thus invisible. This state is successfully attained when the insects, squirrels, and birds in the area no longer take any notice of your presence.

"When striking from above, you can drop on the enemy to crush him with your body weight, and lift him off his feet to render him helpless. One method is to swing off the limb, catching him in a powerful leg-scissors hold about the neck [Figure 75]. By means of this hold he may be lifted and strangled quickly and quietly. Once he is unconscious, drop lightly to the ground and confirm the kill [Figure 76].

"A sentry may be attacked from ambush around a corner with a high degree of success. As in the previous method, people tend to look for what they are interested in rather than 'watching like a hunter' all the time. This tendency may be exploited by concealing yourself below the normal line of

Figure 74. Attacking a sentry from above.   Figure 75.

Figure 76.

sight. The corner of a building or a low boulder, shrub, bush, or tree may be used as the object which screens you from view [Figure 77].

"Again, select a spot where the enemy is at ease, or one that he must pass due to the nature of the trail. Relax and breathe slowly, becoming one with the surroundings. This meditation practice also 'hides the real intent'; that is to say, if one is concentrating on killing, this can be sensed by those with acute powers of perception. If one is relaxed, the victim is less likely to be suspicious or feel uneasy.

"When the sentry passes into range, strike out with a low blow, not above the solar plexus. By keeping below the normal range of vision, you are not likely to be seen until it is too late. A ridge-hand to the midsection, an ankle sweep, or a spinning leg sweep [Figure 78] are excellent means of taking the enemy by surprise and bringing him to the ground.

"Leap to your feet, disarming and immobilizing the sentry for the finishing blow or capture [Figure 79]. A master might be able to save himself by jumping vertically and avoiding such a strike; but a master seldom stands guard duty.

Figure 77. Attacking a sentry from around a corner.

Figure 78.

Figure 79.

"The shallow pit ambush can sometimes be employed in places where no natural or man-made objects are available to provide cover and concealment. Just as a thin layer of earth may be used as a blanket to conserve body heat and provide expedient shelter, so too it may be used to trap the enemy.

"Begin by preparing an area near the trail. Lay aside leaves and twigs on the topsoil. Remember that when such debris is exposed to the air, it dries quickly, so overturned, damp, or discolored leaves and brush indicate that the ground has been disturbed. Scoop out a shallow pit as long as the body is tall and about six to eight inches deep. It is sometimes helpful to select a palm frond or a leafy branch to cover the face and allow one to breathe.

"Lying on the back, cover the body with a ground cloth, or simply hide yourself beneath a thin layer of soil. Atop this, replace such leaves and twigs as are necessary to restore the appearance of natural arrangement. Keep watch by looking down the nose and breathing quietly [Figure 80].

"When the enemy approaches, allow him to pass your hiding place, then suddenly sweep out an arm or leg and knock his feet out from under him to bring him to the ground. Consolidate this advantage by leaping to your feet and applying a control hold or finishing strike [Figure 81, 82].

Figure 80. Shallow-pit ambush.

Figure 81.

Figure 82.

"Again, take advantage of the limited sight radius of the sentry, attacking from beneath the normal range and from an unexpected angle.

"The water ambush is more difficult than many others. The principles employed are also applicable to the trapdoor spider ambush. Essentially, the sentry must pass very close without seeing the agent. When executed in the water, this ambush is sometimes known as raccoon fighting, since it is based on the raccoon's tactic of luring pursuing hounds into deep water and then pulling them under or riding them to drown them.

"There are three common methods of ambushing an opponent in the water: waiting in the water with only the nose above the surface until the enemy approaches, then ducking under to attract his attention and lure him to his death; using a snorkel or breathing tube in order to remain completely submerged until the enemy attempts a river crossing, then attacking him from below the surface; and swimming underwater to attack the enemy as he bathes or makes a crossing.

"From underwater, you may leap up and grab the enemy, depending on surprise to freeze him momentarily, since the sound of rushing water as you surface will certainly attract his attention. The preferred method is the double-ankle pick-up. From below knee level, cup the hands around the ankles of the enemy and push forward with the shoulders to topple him forward. This should disorient and confuse him as well as make him drop whatever weapon he may have. As he falls over, spring to your feet and jump forward onto his back. Secure a hold and continue to pull or push him under until his struggles cease. Water restricts the use of ordinary combat techniques, but, when you work with the medium instead of against it, you will find that the water itself can be used as a weapon.

"Stalking a sentry is not actually a form of ambush, but is traditionally included in the ninjitsu curriculum because it involves stealth techniques. There are many good methods employing the garrote and various other implements, but none are of any use if the Ninja cannot successfully approach his objective; and, as always, it is better to avoid a confrontation than invite one. Still, there are applications for this technique.

"Creep up on the unsuspecting guard or sentry by using the heng pu, or cross step, as it is the most silent and effective for this type of attack [Figure 83]. Initially hold the arms folded across the chest defensively, forming fists with which to strike out should the enemy sense or hear you. Be ready to spring upon him at any moment should he give a sign that he is aware of you. As you advance, cover as much ground as possible to draw near him, and cross-step in front with the rear leg to complete the maneuver and come within striking distance. Open the arms for balance, staying low.

"Strike the enemy suddenly from behind with three attacks: a swinging ridge-hand with the left hand to the throat to prevent an outcry; a thumb or fist strike to the kidney with the right hand to inflict pain and disorientation; and a knee strike to the back of his legs to break his balance [Figures 84, 85].

"Lock the other arm behind his head in the Japanese stranglehold and squat down quickly to break his neck [Figure 86].

"Any weapons confiscated from the enemy soldier should be concealed along the escape route. This permits you, the fleeing agent, apparently unarmed, to fire upon the pursuing party, leading the enemy to overestimate the size of your forces. To reinforce this illusion, each incident of gunfire must be treated as a separate position, fortified and manned. For their own safety, the pursuit team members are obligated to surround and attack each position, having no way of knowing that they are being fired upon only by their quarry, who stops to shoot at them from time to time. This delaying action is also effective if there is actually more than one agent in the field. Each would leap-frog the other from hidden weapon to hidden weapon, providing covering fire and giving the impression of an entire army of agents in support.

"Along the escape route, beyond the periphery of the patrolled areas, an agent might provide barriers and traps to

Figure 83. Stalking a sentry.

Figure 84.

Figure 85.

Figure 86.

ensnare enemy vehicles, although for the most part he would stick to a path which would be difficult for motorized vehicles to follow. Hitting a stretch of heavy, loose gravel around a sharp curve at high speed can be fatal. Mud slides and overhanging obstacles are also hazardous.

"Dig out from under roadways, or direct running water beneath asphalt or concrete, weaken bridge abutments, place obstacles in the road so that the enemy will be forced to stop and clear them. The object is to slow down the posse and increase your chances of escape."

PENETRATION OF SECURED AREAS

"Beyond the necessity of passing through patrolled areas to surreptitiously reach an objective, an agent in the field may further be faced with various barriers around the enemy's perimeter designed to prevent or impede progress through any but authorized checkpoints. Such barriers are numerous, and best addressed in specialized infiltration training, but include barbed wire, steel fences six, eight, or ten feet high, which may be topped with concertina wire or razor ribbon (both are types of barbed wire), as well as high stone walls or barricades. Here we have discussed only obstacles that can be negotiated without special tools. Stockades, forts, and so on also present obstacles to a successful escape and impediments to pursuit. It is more effective to booby-trap the gate to keep a posse in than to try to outdistance your pursuers climbing over the fence.

"Guard dogs may be poisoned, drugged, or distracted. Sprinkling red pepper across the trail clogs the membranes of pursuing bloodhounds.

"Night vision glasses used to scan the perimeter operate by amplification of existing light for visibility. At night the Ninja moves from one point of cover to another just as in daytime, defeating this expedient. Super-hearing devices are also rendered useless by one who practices moving silently, since incidental noises made by insects, wind, wildlife, and so on will mask his approach."

We practiced all that day, rehearsing the techniques of

camouflage and concealment normally reserved for muggers and creepers of the night. Everyone had a turn at playing both attacker and victim. The instructors usually took the victim's part, as well as the falls. Being considerably more adept than the trainees at self-defense, they usually avoided the attack as it was launched, or quickly reversed the situation. This led many to observe that it would be virtually impossible to sneak up on either one of them successfully.

Afterward, we gathered at the lakeside, where we engaged in some mild rough and tumble wrestling, having tested and gauged each other's mettle during the ambush practice, and seen the amount of force permitted by the teachers. Naturally some were more skilled at this than others, and several students preferred to sit out the matches. The latter group was made up almost exclusively of those who had been best at surprise attacks that day.

This was a fact the instructors were quick to point out, so that all of us might feel we had achieved a moderate degree of success, and to demonstrate what they called the general balance of nature. It was late in the afternoon when the camaraderie began to give way to hunger and someone observed out loud that there had been no lunch.

The teachers had us gather beside the lake bank, where they promised to show us how to "live off the land."

FISHING

"Freshwater fish must always be thoroughly cooked," taught the chief instructor, "since they carry bacteria and organisms which may prove harmful or fatal to humans. On the other hand, raw saltwater fish, like Japanese sushi, is considered a delicacy.

"There are many excellent methods of catching and trapping fish, but we shall deal primarily with those methods which employ the staff, as this is the basic tool with which we are concerned.

"First, the staff itself may be sharpened into a spear by vigorous rubbing against a rough stone until a point is achieved. It should be sufficiently slender to pierce the body of the fish. The conical tip may be hardened by slowly rotating it in the fire to dry the wood. While a sharp point may stab and kill the prey underwater, the fish is likely to wriggle free and escape if merely speared. Two methods rectify this: the addition of a thorn or stick facing backward from the tip, which acts to prevent the fish from sliding off once it has passed through; and the simple procedure of pinning the speared fish to the bottom until a hold can be secured with the other hand [Figure 87].

"This also eliminates the problem of having to aim well below the target due to the refraction of the water. The point is held in the water and stabbed down when the fish passes under. Since point and fish are underwater they appear in proper perspective.

"A similar procedure, probably predating the use of stone spearheads and metal tips, is the addition of a frog-gig to an unsharpened staff. The gig is made from a short forked stick, sharpened and hardened as previously indicated, and lashed

Reverse spear tip

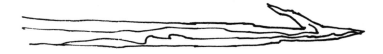

Frog-gig bound to staff

Figure 87. Spears for catching fish.

to the heavy end of the rod. Since it presented more points, it often had a better chance of sticking the target, and can be replaced more easily than one's favorite staff [Figure 87].

"The points are poised over, or as near as possible to, the target, be it frog or fish, and while the forward hand remains rigid, the rear hand shoots the staff forward, much as one shoots a pool cue. Thus, the thrust is very short and much less likely to go astray than if one were using a javelin throw.

"The simplest application of all is to merely club the fish, or stun it with the blunt end in shallow water."

We had arrived at the lakeside from upwind, and so had not initially noticed the strong fishy odor of the pond. This, it was explained, was due to the season. The inhabitants of the retention area were "bedding." That is, the females were fanning out shallow spawning holes along the edge of the lake with their tails, and thereby attracting the males from all over the pond.

Wading knee-deep into the water, the instructor then demonstrated several methods of catching fish barehanded.

"First," he said, "when fishing in saltwater areas, concentrate on tidal pools, where fish may be stranded by the receding tide, or in shallow areas between sand bars. In lake fishing, look for inlets and other places, such as coves and anchorages, where the water is likely to be calm.

"When fishing in freshwater rivers and streams, choose a place where natural obstacles like rocks and sunken logs tend to direct the flow of water and traffic through a bottleneck, or narrowing of the riverbed. In some mountain streams, the water must pass over layers of rock, making it very shallow. Salmon leap over the rocks to return to their spawning ground. At such times they are extremely vulnerable, being often out of water. In the spring, bears frequently feast upon the fish migrating upstream." [Figure 88]

The oldest known fishing technique was learned by observing bears, the chief instructor told us. To demonstrate, he stood leaning over the surface of the pond, staring intently downward, arms hanging loosely at his sides, elbow-deep in the water.

Suddenly, his hands shot out of the water. Between them,

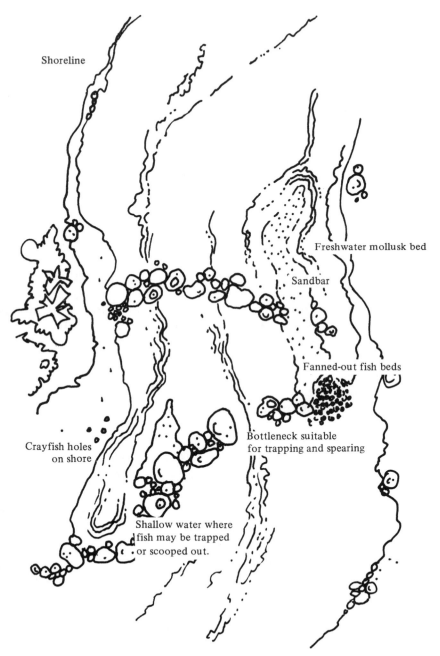

Figure 88. Terrain features for freshwater fishing.

lightly held, was a freshwater bass about ten inches long, probably weighing two or two and one-half pounds. He tossed it easily on the bank, where it flopped helplessly amid the still falling drops of water.

"Usually you don't catch one that quickly." He smiled, returning to his work. It was quite a while before another fish ventured into the area, but eventually, another did arrive. This one was more aptly captured between the grip of the chief instructor's hands, where it could be held inside a small cage of fingers. After displaying it proudly, he returned the fish to the pond—a somewhat anticlimactic conclusion to the long wait for another bite.

The training group was soon divided into parties which gathered the makings of the evening meal. Some were directed to fish, others to search for crawfish, turtles, snake and bird eggs, berries, plums, and anything else that might be considered edible and nourishing. We were also instructed to seek out a secret place, where we would later be expected to retire for solitary meditation. This was, of course, a test of the morning lessons in finding and establishing an overnight base camp.

Other than these simple clues, no requirements were imposed, and the members could range as far or become as elaborate as they felt necessary. The pair of instructors remained at lakeside, identifying plants and lending assistance whenever needed. They seemed to be in no great hurry, nor were they overly demanding of the students' work.

Fish Cleaning

When we were all reassembled, the chief instructor bade us gather round for a lesson in meal preparation. He selected a palm-sized sunfish from the catch of the day, and cradled it between his hands.

"You may have noticed," he began, "that we have used no tools to make our fire or catch our food, other than those which could be made by hand. We have used no knife, since that teaching is reserved for those who learn the way of the sword; but you have heard it said that every finger is a dagger, every hand a sword, and this is true.

"A fish saved my life once," he said, as if remembering some long-ago tale of woe. He gazed upward at the clear blue sky, and then, looking down at us once more, he smiled. "I ate him."

He had been holding the fish belly up. Now his fingernails cut into the soft flesh just below the anus and slid upward into the body of the sunfish. They penetrated fully, and his fingertips, which almost touched in a spear-type point, dipped down and turned inward toward his chest, ripping the fish open. Continuing to rotate, his thumbs came to the back of the fish above the fin, and pushed. In less than a second, the fish had been gutted and turned inside out, the white meat ready to be stripped off the skin and added to the pot. Only a few of us were able to learn this trick.

Of course, the technique requires a knowledge of the anatomy of the fish, as the bones are sharp enough to stab deeply into the hand. The bones should also be avoided when eating, lest they become lodged in the throat or intestine. Some fish have sharp scales, capable of cutting the skin; and the catfish, as well as some saltwater fish, has poisonous spines.

The other items for the stew were cleaned by hand and broken into small enough pieces to be easily eaten and cooked.

COOKING

When the various items which would compose our lunch had been cleaned and prepared, they were assembled on a large sheet of butcher paper which had been brought along, in addition to the paper bags used to make the tea and the tiny paper cups we had been taught to fold using the Japanese art of origami.

The chief instructor compressed the fish and vegetables into a tight package, folding the heavy paper over and around them. This packet was placed into one of the brown bags, which was closed over itself to further wrap and insulate the contents. As we watched, he pointed out that, in cold climates, paper can be used to provide insulation for the chest, hands, and feet.

Some of the students were dispatched to gather a quantity of the soft clay from the bank of the lake. When they returned, the clay was mounded around the entire paper package to form a large brick about two inches thick.

This crude stone oven was lowered into the fire pit, where it rested heavily on the embers. The chief instructor pointed out that the oven method creates less smoke than roasting, and there are no cooking smells to draw large predators which might be lurking in some areas. Cooking time for our meal would be from one to two hours, he said, but the brick could be left in the glowing coals all day. In fact, many an agent would hunt at night and then prepare his meal in this manner. After sleeping all day he would awaken in the evening to a hot meal. Also, the brick could be used to store food for short periods, keeping it safe from insects and bacteria. In Korea, such clay pots, filled with cabbage and fish, are buried in the ground for extended times and allowed to ferment, making a dish known as kimchi. Food left inside the brick in which it has been cooked will keep for a long time, provided the clay is not cracked or broken; the principle is similar to that of canning food to preserve it.

"Cooking," the chief instructor explained, "destroys any harmful bacteria and organisms which may have contaminated the product.

"One useful method of outdoor cooking is roasting. The most familiar example to most Americans is the hotdog on a sharpened stick, held over an open flame until browned or blackened to the diner's taste. This is a very quick way to prepare a meal in the wilderness, scorching the outside of the food and sealing the juices inside. Roasting is equally effective for fish, small game, fruits, and vegetables. The best skewers are metal rods, because they absorb heat and thus speed the process by cooking the food from the inside as the flames cook outside.

"There are various ways to suspend the skewer above the flame so that it may be merely watched and turned every so often rather than held in the hand. Two forked sticks driven into the dirt on either side of the fire make an excellent support on which to hang a shish kebab over the fire; or one can use the crane method, whereby one end of the skewer is jammed under a rock or another heavy object, with the center of the skewer propped in the fork of a single stick, and the tip hanging over the coals. A variation of this method is to put one end of the skewer in the fork and the other under the stone, suspending the meat in the center on the incline.

"In the absence of metal skewers, sticks may be used. They should be clean and dry, since resins and tars may spoil the taste of food. Care must be taken to avoid using sticks from poisonous plants. In the South, where oleander grows wild, people have been fatally poisoned by using its branches as hotdog skewers. The oleander is an evergreen with snowy white or rose-colored flowers in season.

"A diet in the wild is likely to lead to vitamin or mineral depletion or deficiency. An understanding of basic nutritional requirements can help one to avoid this problem, but the best course is to stay on a survival diet for as short a time as possible before returning to a balanced diet."

EATING

"There are three types of eaters in the world," the chief instructor continued. "Those who use knife and fork, those who use chopsticks, and those who eat with their fingers. In the field, because of the desire to employ as few implements as possible, or perhaps because ninjitsu is an Oriental art, the members of this ninjitsu style are expected to be able to improvise eating utensils and feed themselves with chopsticks [Figure 89].

"Finding a pair of twigs to use is not as simple as it might sound when one has no knife. Green wood should never be used. Tree juices and sap may taint the food. Twigs dry enough to permit the bark to be scraped off with a fingernail and to break with a sharp, clean snap are usually sanitary, but check for insects or mold. Twigs about eight to ten inches long and approximately as big around as a wooden pencil are best."

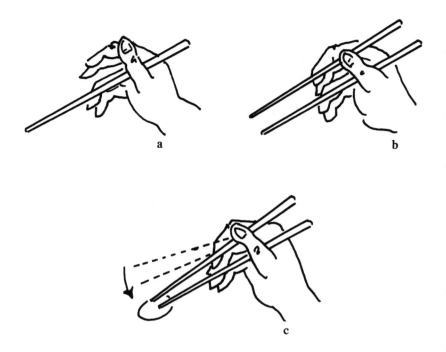

Figure 89. Eating with chopsticks. a) Hold one chopstick in a fixed position in the crook of the thumb. b) Hold the other chopstick like a pencil between the ball of the thumb and the next two fingers. c) Use the top chopstick as a movable pincer to pick up the food.

Having mastered the pincer technique of eating with chopsticks with relative ease, we helped ourselves to the steamed morsels in the earthenware bowl, sipped tea, and nibbled the wild salad and berries that composed the rest of the meal. Eating with chopsticks is an eminently sanitary and efficient way to share a bowl, and chopsticks made from twigs are disposable, thus fulfilling security requirements.

It was night, dark and windy, when the chief instructor once again stood up to speak. We could all see him clearly in the flickering firelight, and, as usual, his voice carried easily to the furthest row.

"We will not be returning to the bunkhouse tonight," he said calmly. This came as no surprise to me. "Instead, we will present a demonstration of our art."

"Why have you come here?" he asked rhetorically. "To become soldiers of the night? Mysterious shadow warriors like those of ancient Japan? Invisible assassins? To wage some never-ending battle for truth, justice, and the American way? To war on occult battlefields against unseen enemies? For some political ideal? Or money?" I half expected him to add, "Or to spy on our organization and report back to our enemies?" thus naming my secret mission. I was glad that he did not, but wondered whether he suspected.

"You have no concept of the years it takes to become a true Ninja," he continued, "and we can offer only a glimpse into that hidden world and an opportunity to practice some of the tricks a few times. Ninja are not supermen; they are more akin to the magicians from whom they are descended, aware of certain natural principles and scientific facts that make it possible to do ordinary things in extraordinary ways. When others see this, they assume the Ninja are possessed of powers beyond the realm of mortal men; and this is so. For each person creates for himself the world in which he chooses to live, and only he can change it. He who limits himself to the mediocre cannot climb higher. We cannot carry you to new heights, for each must walk his own path. We are like the ocean waves, always there to assure or confirm the never-ending cycle of birth, growth, change, and rebirth—no more or less.

"There are those who believe that life here, began out there." He gestured toward the clearing night sky. "Beyond the outer limits of the imagination, among the surging stars of the infinite universe. And this, too, is so. At first there was nothing." He paused dramatically.

"It is the nature of living things to survive. It is also the nature of things to resist change, so transformation must happen slowly. Since life is an endless cycle, there is plenty of time. There is nothing new under the sun, only variations of presentation by those rediscovering the ancient secrets. Therefore, the best we can hope for is to successfully imitate the masters of the way we have chosen."

The chief instructor's voice had taken on a hypnotic quality which encouraged the mind to disregard the blasts of wind and later, as the weather changed, the sighing evening breeze from the lake. While still aware of the world around me, I was not distracted by it and was able to focus on his lecture.

"When a thing reaches its extreme, it begins to come back again," he continued. "This is the law of change, and it is inevitable. Matter retains its state of rest or its velocity along a straight line so long as it is not acted upon by an outside force. This is called the law of inertia. For every action there is an equal and opposite reaction, and this is true of karma; for the good or evil we do will in time be done to us. We know neither the reason for our birth nor the hour of our death. We are aware only of our passage from one to the other, and that each of us must determine the quality of that journey.

"What will happen in your life is already written, but you must choose to be there. You cannot escape your fate.

"There are no extraordinary men, only ordinary men who choose to place themselves in extraordinary situations. Therefore, we use death as an advisor. Whenever we are troubled, we need only turn to our left and look swiftly to see Death sitting calmly, waiting his turn. He will say when the Game is done.

"I am only one and can do little against the forces of nature, so I do not contend against them. I seek to know, so that I may be of service to my fellow-man, and sometimes the needs of the many outweigh those of the few. It is at such times, when the people are oppressed, or liberty threatened, or there is suffering and pain, that the Ninja among us arise in every age to restore balance. I am only one, but because I am one, I must do what I can to prevail in this world and to serve a higher purpose.

"We cannot explain what it is we do nor what we have learned by the practice, only what we have done and the way in which we practice. True knowledge has been passed from master to student in much the same manner from the beginning of time. The hermits shared it with the villagers, who had forgotten the wisdom; the villagers in turn shared it with the city folk, when cities came to be; and from there the knowledge spread from ports throughout the world. Each time it was the same pattern, only different, colored by each master, each student, in his own way. Always changing, yet unchanged for thousands of years."

APPARITION

The chief instructor had been strolling slowly around the perimeter of the flickering firelight, speaking softly and without pause until everyone seated on the hard ground had fallen into a state of utter relaxation. Subtly directing their attention to the fading embers of the campfire, he had fascinated them with the ancient instinct of man to watch the progress of the fire. The gradually diminishing light and the rhythmic singsong of the master's voice worked together to create an atmosphere of hypnotic suspense.

As if he had been waiting for the blaze to die, the chief instructor completed his circuit, returning to his starting point at the northernmost point, and folded his legs beneath him just as the last flame flickered and disappeared. The gusty wind that had punctuated his opening remarks had by now subsided, and the world was still and dark.

He was barely visible in the red glow of the embers, sitting cross-legged, staring into the coals like all the other members of the training class. His right arm swept out in a smooth circular motion to the side. Pausing vertically, edge side of the hand forward, it was lowered down the centerline of his body. Those nearest him later reported that he whispered the word *Shiva* at this juncture. Inhaling as his left hand described a similar arc, and exhaling as it lowered to join the right, he called forth the word *Shakti.* (In Hinduism, Shiva-Shakti is the Godhead. Shiva is the masculine principle, and the destroyer, while Shakti is the Great Mother, giver of life.)

To complete this gesture, both hands performed their movements simultaneously. The heels of the hands came together over his head, and as they lowered in front of his chest, he uttered the word *Shanti,* which was later translated to mean balance, or peace.

His fingertips came together one at a time, starting with the little finger. With each meeting, he muttered the name of one of the elements: earth, water, fire, air, void. As he formed the praying hand gesture, palms flat together, he said, "These are the five elements, whereby all manner of things may be accomplished."

While most of this speech was softly whispered, it seemed that everyone heard it quite clearly. From the last position, the chief instructor's fingers began to knit together to form the nine kuji kiri, until at last he ended with one palm covering the other fist, a mystical way of implying that he possessed some hidden, or occult, knowledge.

Everyone was watching him intently now, yet he appeared oblivious of our presence as a strange mixture of concentration and relaxation seemed to pervade his very being. At first I was not certain whether I heard or imagined the low, vibratting sound which soon filled the area, then I dismissed it as the thrumming of frogs near the water's edge; but after a time I was aware that the sound was that of the chief instructor chanting the mantric word *Om,* thought by the Hindus to be a complete expression of Brahman, the supreme being.

The droning persisted for what seemed to be a long time before drifting off forever on the night wind. With its departure, however, came the renewed stirring of the breeze, which grew steadily stronger, soon becoming a whipping wind.

It has been said of the Druid wizards of old that they possessed the power of calling up a windstorm to destroy their enemies. Often, according to the ancient legends, the priests themselves would be swept away by the fury of the unleashed elements, sacrificing themselves for the destruction of some mighty foe or else bringing about their own destruction by the unholy use of their powers for personal gain.

As the wind whipped and tore at us, I thought a cloudburst must be imminent, but we remained fixed at our posts, watching and waiting for the command to take shelter against the coming onslaught. Sand kicked up in our faces, and the surface of the lake stirred forebodingly. The moon had not yet risen, and I felt the weight of impending doom.

The wind swirled around the chief instructor without harming him in any way and fanned the smoldering embers of the campfire, throwing sparks in every direction. Then, unexpectedly, the fire reignited, bursting into renewed life.

Suddenly, there was light! Enough to see that the instructor was no longer alone at the head of the circle. The instructor sat motionless, as before, his arms loosely draped over his knees, fingers curled around his thumbs. Behind him stood a motionless figure dressed in an ebony garment which covered him from head to toe. Only his eyes were visible, flashing in the firelight through the holes in his full-coverage mask. His stare was intimidating. Over his skintight black hood he wore a faded jacket, of the type commonly worn by martial artists. It must once have been black, but looked as if years of use and laundering had faded it to a dull gray. His forearms extended beyond its shortened sleeves, and he wore the traditional gauntlets which covered only the backs of his hands, leaving the palms free. Around his waist was a well-worn *yudansha,* or black belt, inscribed with several calligraphic symbols and tied in a manner peculiar to ninjitsu. With his hands he made the mystic sign of eternity at solar plexus level.

I noticed some of the others, quick to pick up on the principles of ninjitsu, rapidly counting the number of persons at the party gathering. Yet no one was missing, so it was impossible for someone to have slipped off, dressed, returned to the campsite, and moved behind the instructor to impersonate a stranger. As the light dimmed, it was increasingly hard to see both figures at the same time, as if they were actually one being flowing between two worlds.

Later, discussing the events of the evening, students who were believers in the magic arts would contend that the hooded stranger had been an actual demon summoned from beyond by the chief instructor. The nonbelievers in the group suggested that the incident could be explained away as a case of mass hypnotism. But, for the moment, all of us sat transfixed; for certainly we beheld sensei Ashida Kim. Despite what some said afterward, I'm sure that at the time not a soul doubted that the chief instructor was capable of performing any occult deed or feat imaginable.

The flame died, plunging the group once more into darkness, and where before it had been impossible to discern where the seated figure and the one standing behind him had begun and ended, now we could see only the instructor, sitting as before.

Some, as they later said, felt the presence of other Ninja, circling outside the range of sight.

The demonstration was ended and the audience sat transfixed, mesmerized by the performance. Slowly we came to our senses, eyes adjusting to the glow of the embers and the cold full moon. In a while we relaxed, beginning to breathe normally again.

The chief instructor addressed us quietly.

"Each of you will now go to the places you have selected during the day's training, to wait there until dawn. Then return here for final instructions."

We sat waiting for his handclap we had been trained to expect. Instead he gestured toward the wood; we could barely make it out.

"Go now," he said.

We rose and shuffled quietly off into the darkness, leaving the drill instructor seated at the flames, gently fueling the glowing embers.

There was no approach of any stranger, human or spirit, to the cheery circle of the campfire during the night. Whoever, or whatever, the mysterious performer had been, no one was given any clue as to his identity.

A NIGHT IN THE OPEN

Following the chief instructor's directions, I crept off into the night. I had no idea of the time. My watch was back at the bunkhouse, and all familiar reference had been lost during the dramatic performance which had drawn me deeper and deeper into a web of fantasy and hypnotic reverie.

The silence of moving through the forest at night lent an eerie atmosphere to the evening's events. Far off in the darkness an owl hooted as the cloud cover blew away and the golden moon rose behind the treetops. Moonlight alone made the passage to the hidden place possible.

It was an intensely personal experience. Better to be alone, since the exercise had probed the edges of the psyche; I, along with some others, had wept openly. Such behavior, frowned on in most circles, did not seem shameful here.

I settled into my niche for the night, shoulders to the back of the enclosure, propped in a sitting posture to conserve body heat, beneath a slight overhang to shield myself from the dew which would soon be falling. Ever alert, the mental processes turned to expectations. I wondered what the night would be like; would a meteor flash across the sky, a night-hunting animal stop to impart some message? Perhaps nothing itself was supposed to be of significance.

I sat for a long time. The moon had lowered to the far side of the encircling ring of treetops, and a thick evening mist had risen from the ground and crawled down the gullies and washes. I was only vaguely aware of the stiffness that permeated my body, hunched immobile against the chill early morning air. A feeling that someone was approaching drew my attention. I opened my eyes a slit.

There was a rush of motion through the haze, and a hooded face thrust forward. Coal-black eyes stared into mine, deep into my soul.

The site had been selected because it was hidden, yet this apparition came directly to it without hesitation, as if there were no encumbering mist and darkness. My mind screamed hideously in a futile attempt to react to the threat presented by the starkly penetrating stare of this nocturnal visitor.

Just as quickly, it was gone, swallowed up by the night, only to reappear seated cross-legged little more than an arm's length away. There was an air of humor to his posture, although his face was swathed in black.

"We have been watching you . . ."

The words seemed to echo in my mind, but I did not hear them in the conventional sense of the word. And since the stranger's features were covered, it was impossible to see his lips moving. The misty moonlight and hours of motionless waiting and sensory deprivation from the cold and lack of circulation gave the experience a feeling of telepathic communication.

"You are not like the others," the voice whispered. "You have done well. You have passed all the tests and demonstrated the attributes and skills we require of players in the Great Game."

Though humbled by the praise, I still could not move. The hours of sitting immobile had paralyzed my limbs, making any gesture unthinkable.

"Now you know that ninjitsu is the Way of the Coward. Anyone can hide and strike from ambush. Just as anyone can gather enough followers to make war and impose his will on others, if that be his desire. The trick is to prevail without using force, for the good of all, so that all receive the respect we ask for ourselves, and there is peace everywhere.

"You have traveled far and endured much to reach us, in the hope that we hold the answer to all your many questions and provide some meaning to your quest. We have awaited your coming for a long time. Ask what you want to know."

"Who?" was the question forming in my mind. Even before I spoke, I heard the response.

"I am Ashida Kim," whispered the masked Ninja, "friend to all the world."

Although I had a multitude of queries, here now, in this strange place, in my altered state of consciousness, they seemed meaningless. A feeling of warmth and relaxation seemed to emanate from the weird presence, relieving the morning chill, and I wanted to remain always in his company.

"One must have many teachers, and study many things. In this way, one may learn the truth for oneself. The Game is so designed that when one needs to know a thing, someone, perhaps a teacher, perhaps another seeker, comes to supply the necessary help or information."

"What must I do, then, to become a Ninja?" I asked, or perhaps I merely thought it.

"You must wait. For that is the way of the warrior-mystic. In every age, there are born those with exceptional skill and power, who can affect the course of events and change the pattern of history. We believe you are such an individual, and we would like to have you join us—if you will?"

I managed a feeble nod.

"Very well," the mind-voice replied coldly. "You will be contacted."

In a flash, the mysterious figure was gone! I felt as if I had been held captive by the apparition, as a snake holds its prey by the power of its eyes.

Later, the analytical part of my brain would deduce that the visitor had merely executed a back roll from a sitting position to quickly disappear into the dissipating fog. But, at the moment, the disappearance was as impressive as the entire confrontation and communication had been. It occurred to me that one member of the training staff could have made similar visits to all of the trainees in their isolated cubbyholes, but I soon dismissed the idea since to do so would require a knowledge of everyone's hiding place. Everyone had made a choice freely and alone, and I knew with certainty that I had told no one of the spot I had chosen.

The warming rays of the sun were melting away the enshrouding fog, returning the forest to its ordinary stark reality, when I stirred, stretched, and made off slowly for the base camp.

Day Four

We struggled back into the site of last night's campfire one at a time, looking weary and haggard from the all-night vigil in the woods. Few spoke of what they had seen or heard, and I wondered whether the silent ones considered their experience a secret, too personal to reveal; or had it been so great a disappointment that they were ashamed to tell of their mortification? The chill of the morning air, heavy with the dampness of the nearby swamp, pervaded my very bones, chilling me to the marrow. Everyone seemed eager to return to the lodge.

I was warmly greeted by those who had arrived before me and made comfortable beside the newly built fire, where perked a steaming brew of freshly made tea. We drank in the aroma of the warm liquid long before we were permitted to taste it, and those of us who had begun to understand the Way enjoyed the ceremonious anticipation almost as much as we did the refreshing and invigorating drink itself.

When we had warmed ourselves, some drifted off to sit beside the pond, contemplating the beauty of the serene morning air. Others chatted and joked and spoke in hushed tones of the strange visitation of the night before, as though to talk openly about it would somehow break the spell, leaving them empty and unfulfilled.

I heard the faraway rumble of motorized vehicles long before they arrived to take us back to the lodge.

"Had we been on an actual mission," explained the chief instructor, "we would expect that eventually, friendly forces would arrive in the contested area to provide relief for the advance guard and secure the area. At those times, or when one has successfully evaded the enemy forces through hostile territory and returned safely to his own lines, it would be expected that the agent would not be forced to continue on foot. Therefore, for those who wish to take advantage of this opportunity, we have provided these vehicles."

They were the same vans and trucks which had brought the party from the small airport landing strip to this remote location. The three drivers waved and smiled a greeting from their cabs. Several of the class groaned to their feet and shuffled toward the buses, but the squad leader and the instructors milled about, clearing things away and returning the area to its original undisturbed state. A couple of the students had joined them in this activity, and a few more were beginning the stretching exercises that were preparatory to the morning run.

"Are you coming sir?" called one of those who had boarded a van to the chief instructor.

"In a bit," he replied. "You go on ahead, we'll meet you back at the lodge.

The student looked crestfallen. His smile disappeared as the van lurched forward and carried him away.

"And the rest of you? Anyone else need a ride?" asked the chief instructor as the trucks pulled out.

I had been walking around the campfire site gathering bits of trash that an enemy might find and take as evidence of someone passing that way. Straightening slowly, I said, "If it's all the same to you, sir, I'd kind of like to walk back with you."

The chief instructor smiled broadly.

"Nature is not kind," he said. "But, she is fair. Every day there are tests and lessons and things to do, and only those who can adapt to the pervading environment can and do survive. That is the lesson to be learned here.

"All activity of man may be categorized into two types, survival and conquest. When not actively engaged in one he is most likely engaged in the other. We have shown you that there is more. Some of you have learned it, some have not; just as was promised. And all of you," he swept an arm at the remaining troops, "are changed by the experience; we hope, for the better.

"I speak to you now of friendship. Not the kind so often seen, the shallow, superficial kind that is quickly lost over trivial disagreements or imagined slights, but rather the kind that can only be measured with the heart. For there may come a time when all seems lost and hopeless, and then we have need of an ally who would do as much for us as for himself; who listens not to words, but deeds. And that is what is known as brotherhood."

We had begun to stroll back along the trail, walking in a relaxed and easy manner, listening to these last words of instruction. The group included John, Jake, and Lee, as well as several other students and the two instructors.

"One day, all of you may learn that being a Ninja has to do with controlling one's motion in time and space, not with being powerful or mean, or even invisible. Certainly not with the death and destruction of matter, since neither matter nor energy can be created or destroyed. It may take a lifetime to master one system. Some of us have chosen this one, but all paths lead to the same end. What makes us desire to practice these things, to study and learn, to endeavor in all manner of ways throughout our lives?" he asked rhetorically.

"It is the need to know," he said, answering his own question. "To be of service to others, to set a good example. As the Sage Lao Tsu once said, 'Where should I spend my life and time, but with my fellowman, my long-suffering brothers who do not know any better.'

"We did not refuse the ride back to prove how tough we are, or to make things more difficult on ourselves than need be. Rather, we chose to walk because we are not easily distracted from what we are doing, which is going about the business of being human. Who are we to say that the path chosen by another is wrong simply because it is not the one we have selected? All who are on the road have a creed or code by which they live, determining how they will respond to change and whether they will prevail."

We continued the leisurely strolling pace back to the lodge. John, the student who had chosen not to fight with the pugil sticks, said, "You have told us that there are no extraordinary men. After all the strange and amazing things we've seen—the wasp, lighting the fire by unknown means, and, indeed, many of the things you and the other instructors have intimated during meditation and lecture—are we not to believe from all this that there are in fact what might be called 'magic powers' associated with this system?"

The chief instructor smiled cryptically. "One should never watch a magician too closely," he replied. "Never look up his sleeve, or under his coat. Just sit back and watch his act. Not to duck the issue, however, there are three types of power. The first involves those abilities which may be attained through diligence and perseverance, including yogic techniques of physical mastery. Second is the level of the mind, where dreams are made to become reality, granting radiant good health and, some say, invulnerability to the practitioner. Third is the spiritual level. For one who is aware of the sign of eternity above his head, there are no obstacles; none can resist him. Yet even these levels are but expressions of still higher levels to come. In magic, we say to learn a trick, one must practice an hour a day for one year; so, too, with everything else.

"As Shakespeare's Hamlet told Horatio, 'There are more things in heaven and earth, Horatio, than are dreamt of in your philosophy.'"

Jake ventured a question.

"Will we see Sensei Kim again before we leave?" he asked. Apparently, meeting Kim had been his primary reason for wishing to attend. I wondered whether he too had had a private meeting with the ghostly master.

Jake's question drew a hearty laugh from both instructors.

"And what makes you think you have seen him this time?" taunted the drill instructor.

The pupil said that he had assumed that the stranger at the campfire the previous night had in fact been Ashida Kim.

"No, no," the chief instructor gently corrected him. "Our sensei, Ashida Kim, does not participate in these sessions. He merely checks with us from time to time, to see how things are going. Furthermore, one should never assume anything. The purpose of this class is to teach you to gather intelligence for yourself or someone else. We try to teach you to think as well as act. Never believe anything until it is confirmed by a second source. That is the Way of ninjitsu." He smiled compassionately.

"Kim never speaks, either," he continued; "but, if you're lucky, you might hear him laughing occasionally."

The walk back was all too short, but nonetheless it eased the muscle pains I had developed from sitting, crouching, and lying on the hard, cold ground all night. Also, the easy manner with which we were now treated, more as little brothers than as trainees, led to a certain camaraderie among us. I was more than a bit disappointed when the hike came to an end and we arrived back at the bunkhouse.

The others, who had elected to ride back, sat or lounged casually on the porch, but came swiftly to attention and rejoined the outfit as soon as it was within the grounds proper. The entire party knelt on the packed earth as the instructors made their farewell speeches.

"We would like to thank you all for attending and participating, and we hope that you have enjoyed the experience and learned some of the things you wished to know. If we have been of some small service in this regard, it has been our pleasure," said the chief instructor. The two instructors bowed together.

"Normally at this time," he continued, "had this been an actual operation, you would now destroy all evidence, so that no clue remained to implicate you in any way. This is part of being silent, taking no credit for work that has been done."

There was a look of despair on some faces at these words.

"However," he continued, "since this is merely a training session, and since many of you will be going on to other assignments and more advanced training, we hope that you will carry with you, if not the uniform and boots, at least the bo with which you have trained as a symbol of brotherhood and friendship between us in this world.

"There are no certificates or diplomas, and Ninja are not overly fond of decorating their uniforms with patches and insignia which might reveal their identity or affiliation.

Each of us comes from himself, from his or her own school of life, having no name, no art, which could be used as an indication of philosophy or possible behavior pattern. Each of us is the captain of his own fate, the master of his own soul. You have taken part in a great adventure, you have experienced the awe and mystery that reaches from the inner sanctum of the mind to the outer limits of reality. And your journey has just begun." He looked at us, as he must have looked at so many others he had taught and seen go off to war. We sat raptly before him, drinking in his words.

"In Japan," he continued, very softly, "there is a mountain where, every year, pilgrims come to make the arduous climb to the summit. It is their custom to pause at certain shrines and stations along the way and to mark their progress by inscribing a mark upon the staves they use to help them climb. It is said the view from the top is spectacular and worth the effort of getting there. Go now, pack your things and dress in civilian clothes. After lunch, we will take you to your transport."

The training class rose as a unit and rendered a most humble formal bow to both instructors for their kindness and, in some cases, their harshness. But all of us were grateful for the opportunity to have studied with such teachers.

Some milled about for a few moments after the dismissal, shaking hands with the masters and the other members of the class group, asking questions in an effort to prolong the atmosphere of accomplishment and satisfaction as long as possible. Eventually, all went inside the bunkhouse and followed the instructor's directions, returning to the assembly area shortly before 11:30 A.M.

We were escorted by the drill instructor to the House of Two Moons, where a sumptuous feast of roast beef, chicken, and spaghetti awaited us. Our bellies filled quickly, as our stomachs had shrunk from the enforced lack of food during the previous three days. The drill instructor had changed into a fresh uniform; the squad leader and the chief were nowhere to be seen. We sat around the parlor for most of the early afternoon, enjoying the effects of the hearty meal, and even dozing in the overstuffed chairs.

Each signed out in the large bound volume that was the guest registry of the camp. Then, quietly, in twos and threes, everyone left, shaking hands all around, to be delivered to the airstrip and back to civilization.

I was the last of the trainees to make my departure. Alone in the room, I signed my name in the ledger, then raised my eyes, startled to see the chief instructor lounging in an armchair, as if he had just awakened from a cat nap.

"You were waiting to tell me something?" he asked quietly.

And so, choking with an unaccustomed fear despite his gentle manner, I told him everything: how I had been sent to him as a spy, how during the course of my training I had thought better of my early plans, and had decided to change allegiance. He smiled—a small, inscrutable smile.

"We'll be in touch," he said.

I managed to get outside and catch a ride to the airstrip just as the last van was pulling out.

Afterword

And so we played the Great Game together, perhaps for the last time. It did not matter that there were no rules or dice, no board to romp on; what counted was that we had chosen to participate, learned, and survived.

To what secret identities or separate realities the members of the training group returned upon their departure, or what daring adventures and desperate missions they may have undertaken, we may never know. It has been said, however, that the greater the intellect, the more the need for the relaxation of play, the exercise of the imagination, the fellowship of like minds. So it was that we had stepped out of our normal lives for a short time, escaping into that childlike state where it is permissible to play chase (jogging), follow-the-leader (obstacle course), hide-and-seek (camouflage and concealment), and army (maneuvers, drill, and survival training).

In the process, we learned something about humanity and fieldcraft, as well as the shadowy surreal world of espionage as it has been taught since ancient times to the mystic warriors of the night—the Ninja!

One thing I have never discovered, and suspect that I never *will* discover, despite my desire to learn the truth. When I made my confession to the chief, expecting him to react with anger and shock—why did he look amused? Had he known of my assignment all along, perhaps inviting me to the camp in full knowledge of my reason for applying? If so, he had observed me during my stay, calculating my moves, as a cat watches a mouse. Maybe he had *not* known in the beginning that I came as an enemy into his circle, but had later guessed. Or could it be that no statement I could make, however unexpected, had the power to astonish or disconcert this master of ninjitsu?

Martial Arts Books Ordering Information

Ask for any of the books listed below at your bookstore. Or to order direct from the publisher, call 1-800-447-BOOK (MasterCard or Visa), or send a check or money order for the books purchased (plus $4.00 shipping and handling for the first book ordered and 75¢ for each additional book) to Carol Publishing Group, 120 Enterprise Avenue, Dept. 1558, Secaucus, NJ 07094.

Aikido Complete
by Yoshimitsu Yamada
Oversized 7" x 10", illustrated with step-by-step photographs through-out
$9.95 paper   0-8065-0914-7

Forbidden Fighting Techniques of the Ninja by Ashida Kim
Oversized 8 1/2" x 11", illustrated with step-by-step photographs throughout
$9.95 paper   0-8065-0957-0

From Bruce Lee to the Ninjas: Martial Arts Movies by Richard Meyers, Amy Harlib, Bill and Karen Palmer
Oversized 8 1/2" x 11", illustrated with photographs throughout
$14.95 paper   0-8065-1009-9

Jiu Jitsu Complete by Kiyose Nakae
Illustrated with step-by-step draw-ings throughout
$9.95 paper   0-8065-0418-8

How To Become a Ninja: Secrets From Ashida Kim's Training Camp
by Anonymous
Illustrated with step-by-step photographs throughout
$8.95 paper   0-8065-1558-9

Ninja Mind Control by Ashida Kim
Illustrated with step-by-step photographs throughout
$8.95 paper   0-8065-0997-X

Ninja Secrets of Invisibility
by Ashida Kim
Illustrated with step-by-step photographs throughout
$7.95 paper   0-8065-0920-1

Secrets of the Ninja by Ashida Kim
Illustrated with step-by-step photographs throughout
$12.95 paper   0-8065-0866-3

Ultimate Aikido: Secrets of Self-Defense and Inner Power by Yoshimitsu Yamada, with Steven Pimsler
Oversized 8 1/2" x 11", illustrated with step-by-step photographs throughout
$16.95 paper   0-8065-1566-X

(Prices subject to change; books subject to availability)